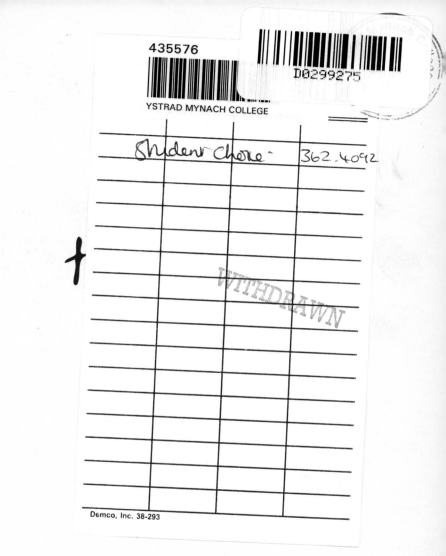

435576

Student Choice - 362.4092

Demco, Inc. 38-293

D0299275

Also by Nicole Dryburgh:

The Way I See It

More from Hodder Children's Books:

Weighing It Up
Ali Valenzuela

Poppy the Dogs Trust Dog
Sophia Fergus

Nicole Dryburgh

Talk to the Hand

Hodder
Children's
Books

A division of Hachette Children's

To my brother, Lee xxx

Contents

Introduction

Don't worry if you read my first book, there are no rules for this one, seeing as most people broke the rules for reading *The Way I See It* (TWISI)!

If you've read that book, then you'll know that my life is quite eventful, so this is a follow-up to tell you everything that's been happening since the end of TWISI.

For those of you who *haven't* read TWISI, here is a short, and I mean very short, version of my story . . .

I was diagnosed with a rare type of cancer, called a peripheral nerve sheath tumour, when I was eleven years old. I had most of the tumour removed from the top of my spine, followed by eight weeks of daily radiotherapy. I then went into remission. Two years later, at the age of thirteen, I had a brain haemorrhage, and spent three months in hospital. During that time I also had a stroke, slipped into a coma, lost my sight due to lack of oxygen to my brain, and as a result of nerve damage to my spine, I'm now disabled.

The brain haemorrhage was caused by an engorged blood vessel on my spine bursting and travelling to my head. There had been another tumour underneath a ball of blood vessels which we hadn't known about. I then started chemotherapy, which I had in tablet form at home, but was told I only had a couple of months to live. Luckily though, that proved not to be the case, and I finished my chemo in February 2004, ten days after my fifteenth birthday. I was then in remission for the second time.

But when I was seventeen, I relapsed from my cancer again, and had to undergo a much tougher course of chemotherapy which I had to have intravenously this time, and stay in hospital for it. The treatment finished just after my eighteenth birthday and that's where this book picks up from, so you will read about what's happened since then.

I'm often asked how I cope, and to be honest, I don't really know. It's not a case of: I do this and then that, and that's how I get through it – I just don't see any other way *but* to cope. I believe in making the most of what I've got, whatever the situation. I can't change the past, but I can try and make the future go the way I want it to, so that's what I try to do.

I'm lucky that I'm so stubborn (although other people might not agree!) – that's what helps me get through everything that's thrown at me. Well, that and Tetley tea! I may as well admit it now, I'm addicted to Tetley. Not very good for the street cred of a twenty-year-old, but it just tastes so nice! Anyway, my stubbornness and determination won't let anyone or anything get the better of me or stop me from doing something, and I have a very matter-of-fact approach to life, so I think that's why I'm able to just get on with things.

In this book, along with updating you on my life, I've included some of the things I do to get through the problems that come with it. I hope that in some way that might help you, too. I'm a self-confessed moody cow – I just can't help it – so I have many ways I cope in different situations. Which strategy

I use for coping depends on my mood, the circumstances and where I am. Some of my strategies are a bit strange – as you'll soon find out – but they work for me, so hopefully some will work for you too.

O N E

Remission Accomplished!

Three days after my eighteenth birthday in February 2007, I had my sixth and final course of chemotherapy. I had the usual kidney test and echo scan of my heart beforehand to check the damage from the previous round of chemo, and they showed that the final round had to be reduced quite a lot because my body wouldn't have been able to tolerate more. I was just grateful to have that final round, anyway – I didn't care how much chemo I had to have, I just wanted it to work.

So on Thursday 15th February 2007, I finished my chemo at around 9.30 a.m., and Linda (my auntie) arrived at 10 a.m. to take Mum and me home. Just before that, though, the nurse checked my Hickman line and said the skin round it looked red and could be infected. She said they would get me some special bandages to put on it, but that they needed to be signed for by a doctor. They were also just sorting my medicines to take home, and those too needed to be signed for by a doctor.

An hour passed, then another, and I was getting very stressed and frustrated, and just wanted to get home. After another hour, I said to Mum in a very stroppy tone, 'Right, that's it, we're going.'

'We have to wait for the nurse with the bandage,' she answered.

'I don't want the stupid bandage,' I snapped back.

'Well maybe you'd like to say that to the nurse who's standing in the doorway right now holding the stupid bandage,' Mum replied.

So I just mumbled, 'Well hurry up with it then,' and burst into tears. God, chemo did make me emotional!

We finally left the hospital at about 3 p.m., and once we arrived home a couple of hours later, I was then happy.

But just because my chemo was over, it didn't

mean I wasn't still affected by it. My fingernails started to split and peel off, which was horrible. I had six white lines on my nails from each round of chemotherapy – they'd stop growing while I had the course of chemo, then start growing again once it had finished and my body began to repair itself.

For about two months, every time one of my nails started to grow it would break, and all my nails were really soft and would just peel away. They split across the middle of the nail too, which could be painful, but they're now strong again and back to normal. My hair soon started growing back after the treatment, which was brilliant, except that my eyebrows needed major waxing and reshaping as at first they just grew back as one big hairy caterpillar above my eyes! Luckily, they're under control again now. Phew! The two parts of my body I love the most are my nails and eyebrows – I always have to have them perfect – so to lose both of them was tough.

The way chemo works is by attacking the living cells in your body, as cancer is a cell which constantly grows out of control. Chemotherapy is designed to kill the out-of-control cells in your body, and that's why things like your hair and nails are affected, because they're living cells too, and chemo can't tell the difference between good and bad living cells. It just kills them all.

This should help give you some idea of what going through chemotherapy is like. If you imagine that everything in your body that wants to live is being killed, whether it's good or bad, you're not being allowed to develop and grow properly. Every time your body picks up after a course of chemo and starts to function again and you feel better, that's when you get hit with another course of chemo – because when your good cells grow again, so do the bad. Chemo means months and months of going through hell, and unless you've been through it, you really don't know how bad it is. I'm not trying to be dramatic about it (or scare you), simply explain honestly what it's like.

I would say, however, it's an experience I would never – ever – change, because having cancer makes me who I am, and although my body might not have been growing, I certainly grew as a person.

Less than a month after my chemo finished, I had my Hickman line, AKA *Mr Wiggly*, removed. This tube was put into my chest and stayed there throughout my chemo treatment. It was in a vein, and it meant not having to have needles stuck into me, as all the chemo and other drugs could go through it, and blood could be taken from it. Hickman lines are supposed to stay in for about three months after the end of treatment – to make sure things are well and the treatment's worked – but because I kept getting infections in my line, they took it out as an emergency. In one way, it was great to get rid of *Mr Wiggly* – it meant I could move again without panicking that I'd pull it out; but it also meant going back to having needles stuck in me which I hate (you'll find out all about my needle phobia later). I had an operation under general anaesthetic to remove *Mr Wiggly* and thankfully it didn't hurt too much afterwards – and I'm left with only a tiny scar.

And that, for now, is where my journey with cancer ends. We don't know if it will always end here, but hopefully it will. I'm just going to take each day as it comes and appreciate it, because that's what life's all about.

Tips If You're Feeling Down

These are some of the things I do if I'm having a down day and need cheering up.

Drink a cup of tea

Ah, Tetley. This actually helps in any situation. I always turn to Tetley whatever mood I'm in. It can help in most situations, especially if there are biscuits involved! I find if you're feeling down, drinking something hot that warms you up can really help. Or maybe it's just that I'm addicted to Tetley . . . If you don't like tea or coffee, then try hot orange or hot Ribena. It's lovely!

Top 3 things to eat with a cuppa:

1. Good old-fashioned shortbread. You can't beat it, especially the chocolate chip ones.

2. Chocolate digestives or custard creams dunked in. Don't dunk them for too long though – soggy biscuits at the bottom of the mug is not a good look.

3. Cake, the bigger and more chocolaty, the better.

Get writing

This might only help me because I'm an author, and I love it, but writing can really make you feel better and get your feelings out. I write everything on my pink talking laptop. It's a normal laptop with a speech programme, so it says out loud every key I press. It has a male American accent and I call him

Jeffrey! I do it whatever mood I'm in and it influences what I write. If I'm happy and in a cheeky mood I like to write my online diary on my website at www.c-h-o-c.org.uk, but when I'm down I like to write poems and song lyrics. It helps me express how I'm feeling, and some of my best work has been written when I've been feeling down because it's come from the heart – cheesy but true. I find it hard to say out loud how I'm really feeling, so writing it down makes me feel as if I've actually told someone. I know that might sound stupid, but it helps me, so I'd recommend it to you.

Top 3 things to write:

1. Poems – and I don't care what people say, a poem is not a poem unless it rhymes!

2. Songs – I'd love to become a songwriter one day. I've been writing song lyrics since I was sixteen, so have quite a lot now. You never know, you might hear one of my songs on the radio one day soon!

3. My diary – I have two. The one I let

people see on my website, and the one I don't let anyone read but keep for myself. It's a good record of your journey and it's amazing how your life and feelings can change from year to year. I'd recommend people to read back their old diaries and have a good laugh.

Pamper yourself

Again, whatever your mood, whatever the situation, nothing can make you feel better than a good old pampering session. From a nice hot Radox bath (good for those aching muscles) to soaking your feet in a bubbly bowl of water or putting on a face mask, painting your nails, massaging your feet . . . the list goes on. It will make you feel all relaxed and refreshed, plus a lot cleaner and nicer too!

Top 3 ways to pamper yourself:

1. A nice hot bath. The Body Shop is the best shop for pampering stuff I think, and they have great smells too. Best of all though,

The Body Shop doesn't test their products on animals, so it's one of my favourite shops.

2. A face mask – the peel-off ones are the best and a lot more fun than the other kinds too. It's like you're peeling your skin off!

3. A manicure. I love having my nails done (well apart from the filing part!). I've been having my nails done for years, and I've had all sorts of things on them from foils and glitters, to diamantes and pictures. I've even had my nail pierced once, although it wasn't that good because the nail ring caught on everything. It looked great though!

Hug a hot water bottle

This is like an actual hug, but a lot hotter and without the arms! I use hot water bottles quite a lot as it helps with my back and knee pain. It's often more effective than paracetamol! I don't recommend hot water bottles in the summer though (or if you're made of chocolate), but for best results, wear your pyjamas and slipper socks and be in bed with a cuppa. Ah, cosy.

Top 3 things to wear while hugging the bottle:

1. PJs - the bigger, baggier, fluffier and pinker the better.

2. Your duvet - nothing is as cosy!

3. Fluffy slipper socks - I just love them.

Be creative

This is one of my favourite things to do when I'm feeling a bit down, or feeling ill or just having a quiet day. It gives me something to focus on. I like making cards the most, and send many of them to the children on www.postpals.co.uk, a fantastic website featuring lots of poorly children. The aim of the site is to 'post a smile on a sick child's face', and each of the children, called 'Pals', has their own page with their details, interests, updates and a forwarding address, and people can send them a letter, card, gift or email to make them smile while they're feeling ill. I used to be a 'Pal', and received letters, cards and presents from around the world including America, Australia and Singapore. I like making other things too as I've always been into art and crafts, so it's something I always enjoy doing.

Top 3 things to make:

1. Cards – I think they're a lot nicer and have more meaning when they're handmade.

2. Cakes – doesn't really need an explanation, does it? They taste great!

3. Trouble!

T W O

Bloody Hell!

I don't know why, but I always chart my pain by asking myself if I could go through it again. If I think yes, then it means it can't be that bad, so I shouldn't moan about it. It's just my weird way of thinking.

I've been through some pretty painful stuff over the years, but there have been two experiences which I really couldn't go through again. They are: falling off a horse flat on to my back and knocking myself unconscious; and having another blood clot. I thought the clot I developed in my right arm after my third round of chemo (at the end of 2006) was painful, but that was nothing – and I mean *nothing* – compared to the one I developed two months later.

It was 19th February 2007, and I woke up with a sore right knee and hip. It was like a dull throbbing pain, and it was getting worse and worse; then at about 2 p.m., my leg just exploded with pain. I've never felt anything like it. I knew instantly it wasn't one of the usual spasms I get in my legs, and that it felt like another blood clot. When Mum looked at my knee, it was a mottled blue colour. I kept getting spasms in my leg which was making it even worse. Mum phoned the community nurses, and they said to take me to my local hospital.

I couldn't stand on my leg, and I was sobbing in pain, so Mum phoned for an ambulance. She explained the situation and that we thought it was a blood clot. They asked if I was still breathing, and Mum replied *yes*. They then said they didn't class it as an emergency, and we would have to get to hospital ourselves. Mum didn't want to set off with me on a forty-five-minute drive to the hospital in case I got worse in the car. She asked the person on the phone what to do if I felt really ill on the way there, and they told her she should pull over and call an ambulance.

Honestly, it makes you want to scream!

Well, I was screaming at the time anyway, because of the pain, and the person on the phone must have heard me because practically the whole street could, but still they wouldn't send an ambulance.

Mum then had to struggle getting me out of bed, into my wheelchair, down the ramp outside and into the car. I hadn't got dressed yet because I was having a lazy day – it was only four days since my chemo had finished, so I wasn't feeling that great to start with. I remember I was wearing a blue nightie with a mouse on it eating a piece of cheese, and saying 'midnight munchies'; a pair of yellow three-quarter-length PJ bottoms; a pink cardie; a pair of black fluffy slipper socks with pink toes and heels; and my wig. I looked like a right hippy, but I didn't care!

We arrived at my local hospital, and by this point, my leg was swollen. I'd hurt my ankle getting out of the car trying not to stand and put pressure on it, but I just ended up hurting it even more, so my leg was absolute agony by then.

I was seen by a doctor who I hadn't met before. She asked Mum if I was in pain, so Mum looked at me and asked, 'Nicole, are you in pain?' I replied *yes,* but the doctor didn't seem to take this as a hint that I could answer my own questions and she continued to ask Mum *How old is she?* etc.

This really wound me up; especially as she was asking irrelevant questions like *How many tumours does she have?* and all about my history, which she could get from my notes. She didn't seem to be bothered that I was saying it was a clot in my leg. She tested my reflexes for ages, which involved hitting my leg and ankle (the one with the suspected clot) with a rubber hammer thing.

She even asked Mum if I was wearing a wig. *What that had to do with anything, I don't know!* I think maybe she asked though because my wig had got twisted from me moving my head from side to side listening to the doctor ask the question, then listening to Mum on the other side asking me the same! I had to bite my lip the whole time the doctor was in the room.

One of the last questions she asked was if I had any siblings. Mum replied a brother, then the doctor asked, 'The same father?' I was so shocked. I could be dying of a blood clot, and she was basically asking if my mother was a tart! (She's not by the way!) She rather wisely left after that. Another doctor came in and asked Mum a question, and Mum then turned to me to ask the same thing. The doctor took the hint and asked *me* the questions from then on. It was so much easier!

I was sent for an X-ray, but that didn't show anything. The blood test results showed that there was a clot though. Everyone was confused because I'd been on anti-clotting injections every day since the clot in my arm in December 2006, and they were supposed to prevent another one from happening. I suppose my body's like me though – it doesn't do as it's told! I had an ultrasound of my leg the next day which involved pushing quite hard on my leg with a little monitor covered in jelly. It revealed a blood clot from above my hip to below my knee – and I haven't exactly got short legs! No wonder it bloody hurt!

I also had to have an ultrasound of my liver, spleen and kidneys to see if there were any clots there, and I had a VQ scan to check the blood and air supply to my lungs, which I'd never had before. It involved breathing in some kind of special air from a mask, which I didn't like because it reminded me of being put to sleep under general anaesthetic. I then had images taken of my lungs to see if I had any clots there. I had radioactive dye injected and more images taken, and luckily that showed no more clots.

I spent over two weeks in hospital and it was the lowest point of my treatment. I had never felt so fed up, and if I could have walked out of the hospital, I would have. There's only so long you can put up with uncooked food and patronising nurses who give you no respect or dignity. I had been staying there on and off for several months when I used to get infections in my Hickman line, but everything about it was bad. I was sooooooo glad to come home, and luckily after that I never had to stay there again.

In August 2007, I finally stopped having the anti-clotting injections. In total, I had 246 injections, and I have no idea how I coped with that. We were running out of space on my leg to inject where there wasn't a bruise. Sometimes when we were out I'd have the injection in my stomach – I wasn't getting my leg out in public! We also tried injecting in my back a couple of times as a doctor recommended it and said we shouldn't always inject in the same area, but that really hurt and bled whereas the others only bruised. Mum was the one who used to inject me – very brave lady! I wasn't happy about her doing it at first, but it turned out to be the best thing. She was better than most of the nurses at it, plus it was nice to always have the same person rather than never knowing who'll do it at hospital and if they'll be any good. It was a relief to stop the injections, but a big worry at the same time. For a couple of months after stopping them, every twinge of pain in my leg made me panic and I kept asking Mum to check what colour my leg was, and if it was blue, because I was paranoid about getting another blood clot, but eventually I forgot about it and stopped worrying. I still get funny feelings and pain in my leg now, but I suppose I'll always get that, and I'm able now to tell the difference between just a twinge and a major problem. Fingers crossed that that's the end of the blood clots.

After finishing my chemotherapy, and recovering from the blood clot, I was able to attend college regularly. I had relapsed a few days before I was due to start college, so I had missed practically all of the first five months. I was attending Canterbury College to do an English GCSE, as I hadn't taken any exams after I left my secondary school when I had my brain haemorrhage. I wanted to do an English course because I'd like a career in writing.

I went once a week for three months before the exams took place. Sometimes I went for an extra lesson a week to make sure I understood all of the work. Shakespeare can be quite difficult to get your head around! I had a support teacher who would come to the lessons with me and write down notes, and then email them to me at home so I could revise with the help of Jeffrey (my talking laptop). I managed to catch up with the coursework, which I got a top A for (above an A, but below an A*), and I got an A* for a presentation I gave on Demelza House, a children's hospice I used to go to.

I'd found out a few months before the exams that I had been submitted for the lower exam with the rest of my class, which meant that a C would have been the highest grade I could get. I wasn't happy about that because when I do something, I aim for the top and to do my best, so knowing that I couldn't get the best result made me not want to do it. I asked to change to the higher exam, and luckily I was allowed. It meant the exams were harder, but it's what I wanted to do.

I took the exams in a room on my own, with my support teacher and another teacher. My support teacher read the questions to me and I typed up my answers on Jeffrey. I was allowed double time to do the exams, plus rest breaks, which was great and helped a lot, but it meant that both of my exams lasted over five and half hours. It was a very long time to concentrate, and by the end my back was in a lot of pain, so I couldn't wait for them to be over.

I received the results a couple of months later, and I got a B grade. I was pleased with that, but also really annoyed because I was only five marks below an A! I considered going back that year to do more exams, and looked into some courses, but none of them were suitable or I didn't have enough qualifications to do the course. Plus I was having more problems with my health, so I decided not to go back.

More Tips If You're Feeling Down

Go shopping!

Go on a spending spree. You don't have to spend that much, but it's bound to cheer you up, and if it doesn't, at least you've got out the house for a while and now have a new wardrobe! Also, sort through the clothes you don't want or wear any more and take them to a charity shop. It helps raise money for a good cause, and it's a great excuse to go shopping to fill your wardrobe back up again!

Top 3 shops:

1. Topshop.

2. Topshop.

3. Um, Topshop.

Listen to music

I used to love listening to music before I lost my hearing, and it's one of the things I miss the most now that I'm almost completely deaf. I can't listen to music any more because my hearing is so bad that I can't actually hear it properly, and it just sounds like a load of noise. When I did have my hearing though, I loved songs where I could relate to the lyrics, and I listened to different types depending on my mood.

Top 3 singers:

1. Lemar – simply just lovely!

2. Paolo Nutini – brilliant voice, unique and

very Scottish. It doesn't get much better than that.

3. Christina Aguilera – amazing singer and I love the lyrics to her songs.

Amazing animals

I love animals to bits, and without a doubt, my gorgeous dogs, Molly and Daizy, have helped me through everything. I love just cuddling them, and they always seem to know when I'm down and they'll come and give me a hug. Yes, dogs can hug too you know! Molly helped me through everything after my brain haemorrhage (we didn't have Daizy at the time). She even travelled two hours every week to London to see me in hospital (with the help of my auntie – Molly's clever, but not that clever!). And then when I came home, she sat on my bed right by my side, and she's never left it since – literally! And now she's joined by the adorable crazy Daizy.

Nicole and Daizy

Top 3 animals:

1. Dogs – not just man's best friend, but everyone's! They're forever loyal, loving and never let you down.

2. Monkeys, especially orang-utans and chimps. I've been in love with monkeys since I was eleven, and think they're brilliant.

3. Rabbits – I love their ears and the way they hop! I used to have two rabbits, Womble and Nutmeg, and they were lovely. They're a great animal to hold and stroke too, I think.

Smile :)

It might be the last thing you want to do, I know it often is when I'm in a mood, but just try to smile. Remember, a smile is a curved line that straightens things out, so try it and it might help . . .

Top 3 things to make you smile:

1. The colour pink - so pretty!

2. A camera!

3. This book!

Be positive

Even if you're feeling negative, still try to be positive. Remember there's always someone else out there far worse off than you. I tell myself that all the time and it stops me feeling sorry for myself. Don't look at the bad stuff in your life, look at the good. You can't find any? Look harder. If there's one thing I've learnt from every bad thing that's happened to me, it's that there is always a silver lining. You just have to look for it.

Always look forward, never look back. You can't change the past, so don't try, just make the future what you want it to be.

Top 3 things to be positive about:

1. Life, no matter what it feels like. Appreciate you've got it – and think about the good things in it. You're probably luckier than you realised.

2. The miracle of breathing. A bit cheesy, but as long as you're still breathing, you have something to live for.

3. The fact that someone invented chocolate. A pure genius.

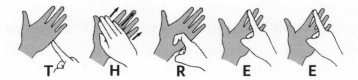

T   H   R   E   E

Hearing Heartbreak

As soon as one problem ends, another begins! But the one I'm about to explain is probably the biggest thing I've ever had to deal with . . .

I first noticed a problem with my ears in January 2007, a month before my chemotherapy finished. I was in my local hospital due to an infected Hickman line, which I often got after each round of chemo. I had an agonising pain in my left ear. It was so bad that it made me cry, and you know it's serious when that happens. I saw three doctors who didn't know me, at three different times, and they all basically said nothing was wrong. One said there was a lot of earwax, but just to leave it, another put cotton wool in my ear and said that would help, and the third gave me paracetamol which was supposed to help ease the pain, but it didn't. I then noticed that I couldn't hear things as well as before. I didn't realise how bad my hearing had deteriorated until I was on the phone one day. I normally hold the phone to my left ear, but for some reason during the call, I swapped it to my right ear (I think it could have been a long call and my hand was aching!). The difference was amazing, and it was then that I realised there was a real problem with my hearing.

I saw my paediatrician in April that year, and Mum said to him that she was scared that I would go deaf, just like she had watched me go blind. He said that wouldn't happen, yet my hearing seemed to still be getting worse. In desperation I tried eardrops to see if that would get rid of the earwax and maybe solve the problem, but it didn't help at all. I saw my paediatrician again in July and he finally referred me for a hearing test, and that showed I had a severe hearing loss in my left ear and a slight hearing loss in my right. I also had my ears cleaned out, which was horrible, but that didn't make a difference. So I had an MRI scan the following month which revealed I had a small tumour in each ear called acoustic neuromas. I then saw an ear, nose and throat specialist who said to do nothing and come back in six months' time to see what my hearing was like then. Well I'm sorry, but I couldn't just sit back and do nothing. I was already totally blind, and now had only half my hearing left, so I contacted the one doctor I can rely on to listen to me properly, Darren, my oncologist at the Royal Marsden Hospital. I went to see him, and it was so nice to have someone listen to me and agree to do something to help. I had lots of appointments over the following two months to discuss what was the best thing to do. Normally they would leave it and see what happens, which is what the ENT specialist wanted to do, but because of my situation, they didn't want to risk me losing the hearing that remained in my right ear. The two options to treat the acoustic neuromas were surgery and radiotherapy, and both carried risks. We decided on radiotherapy as that seemed to be the best option for me.

To prepare for the treatment, I had a CT and MRI scan to plan exactly where the radiotherapy rays would go. They shape the rays to the exact size of the tumour so that it only kills the cells they need to. To ensure that you don't move you have to be

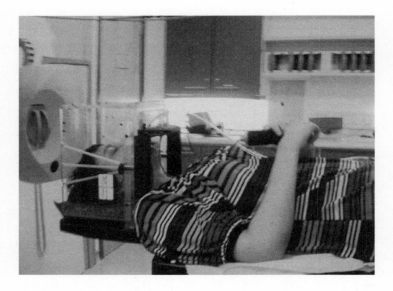

attached to the table. Last time they made a mask of my face and I was lying face down. As it was screwed to the table there is no chance of you moving. This time I had a mould made of my teeth, it was like wearing a gumshield only it was attached to a big metal frame that was then screwed to a bracket on the table. I would lie facing the ceiling in the exact same position for every radiotherapy session and there is no chance of you moving your head. Having the mouthpiece made was really uncomfortable and it left me with a big blister on the roof of my mouth. I dreaded the thought of having to lie like this for every session, but luckily it wasn't as bad as I thought it would be. My mouth kind of went numb after a week of having treatment, so wearing the hard plastic mouthpiece became easier. It was sore on the roof of my mouth where the edge of the plastic mould would dig in, and that's why it always left a mark. A suction pump was attached to the mouthpiece so that it could suck out the saliva and make it really secure. This of course made it stick to the roof of my mouth even more.

I started six weeks of daily radiotherapy at the end of November 2007. The acoustic neuromas are classed as a brain tumour, so it made the situation much scarier. I only had radiotherapy on my right ear, which was the ear I could hear the most out of as I had about 30 per cent hearing left in it. My left ear by this point had less than 10 per cent hearing left, so there wasn't much point in having it on that ear too. After the first two weeks of treatment, the days just seemed to pass quickly, which was good. The worst part was the four hours travelling from Kent to Surrey and back every day, which made me feel really tired and want to sleep all the time. I had a few sore throats and ulcers in my mouth, but apart from that, it wasn't too bad. I was just glad that something was actually being done. My radiotherapy continued over Christmas, but luckily I was allowed Christmas Day, Boxing Day and New Year's Day off, and the treatment finished on 7th January 2008.

Unfortunately, the radiotherapy didn't seem to help, and by six weeks later, I was almost completely deaf. The way to describe being deaf and blind . . . indescribable. It really is the most scary, unreal and emotional feeling ever. It's something I've found very hard to deal with and this is mainly because I couldn't get anyone to listen to me from the start. Who knows? If they had, maybe I might not be so deaf. That's something I now have to live with.

It all came to a head the day before my nineteenth birthday in February 2008, when Mum kind of flipped her lid because no one would help and they didn't know how bad the situation was because they wouldn't listen to us. Mum's normally very chilled and calm (I'm the drama queen in our house), but she had got to the stage where she'd had enough. The months and months beforehand of everything that had, or rather hadn't, happened was too much. It was after Mum flipped that people started doing things to help, and we found out that there were a load of people and gadgets that I could have had to help me, but by then it was too late. There was meeting after meeting, which normally lasted several hours. It involved me sitting in a room full of people and having no idea what was being said. It began to really do my head in. Everyone suddenly wanted to help – telling me to do this, telling me to do that, saying what was best for me – but no one actually asked *me* how I was feeling about it, and it was all just too much. I became a miserable moody cow, and I didn't want to see or speak to anyone. I became very quiet and I wasn't the same person. It was my way of dealing with it.

Talk to the hand

I had to learn how to live as a deafblind person. I learnt the manual deafblind sign language, which in a way has been my lifeline. Deafblind signing works by the person touching a different part of my hand in a certain way for each letter of the alphabet, and spelling out what they want to say. For example, the signer sweeps their right hand over/across the palm of my left hand for the letter **H** and touches the top of my middle finger for the letter **I**. (See diagram opposite.) Now you can all say 'hi' in deafblind sign language! There's a chart of the full manual deafblind alphabet on page 169 – for those of you who want to give it a try.

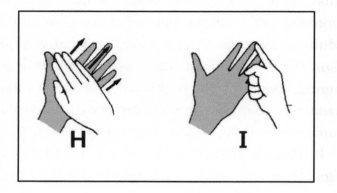

I learnt it quickly, in less than half an hour, because at primary school a friend had taught me deaf sign language, and it was one of those things that you learn and never forget. Deafblind sign language is a bit different, because it's all done on one hand rather than two, but quite a few of the letters are the same sign so it helped to already know some of it. It can look quite difficult, but it's actually very easy once you've learnt it, honest!

I started to have lessons where I learnt signs for different things such as animals, food, colours etc., but after a few sessions I asked to stop because I found them too frustrating. I just kept thinking to myself, I'm nineteen and being taught to put my hands upright on each side of my head and wiggle them for the sign for a donkey, I really don't need this right now. I was still really struggling emotionally, so I didn't have any more lessons. Plus Mum and I found it easier to just make up our own signs for things, and we sometimes do object signing, which is where something is put in my hand such as a mug, and that means, do you want a cup of tea. Clever, huh?

It was decided once I'd learnt the deafblind sign language, that it would help if someone accompanied me to places to sign what people are saying and what's going on – basically be my eyes and ears. What a job! I knew the perfect person – Nikki. I'd known Nikki for over three years as she used to be a carer at Demelza House, but then left to go back to her previous job of working with deaf children, but we stayed in touch. Because of her job, she already knew the deafblind sign language, so when I asked her if she would like to be my guide-communicator, she said yes. She comes practically everywhere with me now, and we have great fun! Whether I'm at a hospital appointment, party, meeting or whatever, she listens to what the

Nicole's mum, Jackie, signing to Nicole

person's saying, then signs it on my hand. We have our own signs for things, and I'm used to the way she signs, and she knows the look on my face now when I pretend I know what she's said but I really haven't got a clue! It can be hard to concentrate on the signing sometimes, especially when I'm tired. Luckily Nikki knows what I'm like now so she'll sign slower or repeat things in those situations. We work together really well. Most people know now that I don't come on my own to places, there's three of me – me of course, Mum and Nikki. Mum and Nikki are the best signers because they do it all the time. Lots of other people have now learnt it too, which I'm really grateful for. I can tell the difference between people by the way they sign. Everyone has their own style of doing it and I know who's signing because of certain little things such as the speed or the way they sign a certain letter or spelling.

My best friends – The Girls – are good at signing too. Mum taught them the sign language when I became deaf and they were some of the first people to learn it. They each chose a sign to indicate that it was them speaking to me. For example, if Charlotte was signing, she would put a little make-up brush in my hand first so I knew it was her, then she'd sign what she wanted to say. Or Nicola would put her sign in my hand – a little tin of Vaseline – before she 'talked' to me. Kerry was a bracelet and Rachel was a bunch of car keys. I know these signs are a bit random, but it was things they always had on them so that they never forgot them. We don't use those signs any more as we're all better at the signing now, and I know the difference between the ways each of The Girls sign, but it helped at the beginning.

We're all very busy these days either with university or work, but The Girls and I still meet up whenever we can. We tend to spend most of the time down the pub now! Drinks, cheesy chips and juicy gossip make a great night out! Obviously The Girls use the deafblind sign language to talk to me, so it's great as no one else can hear the gossip!

I got hearing aids to try and help me hear a bit more, but like everything, it didn't run smoothly. It was several months and several appointments before I got a pair of hearing aids that actually worked properly, but even then they didn't really help. I then went to a different hospital where I was fitted for another pair of aids and these ones were a lot nicer. They were smaller and more comfortable, plus they came in different colours so I got sexy pink ones! I kept trying them but found it very frustrating. Every time I put them in my ears they made me want to cry. They didn't help and actually made things worse because they just magnified *all* noise, so I still couldn't hear voices properly because I could hear all the background noise too. It was then decided after several months, appointments and hearing tests, that hearing aids wouldn't help me, so I stopped wearing them. The problem is that because of where the tumours are in my ears, they distort the words going in. So when people talk at normal speed, I only hear every other word because it takes a while for the words to go in and register. We've now learnt that people have to speak slowly so that each word has time to register with me. It can be annoying and takes ages to have a conversation, but it's the only way I can hear if I don't use deafblind sign language.

I was also advised to start learning Braille again. If I lost my hearing completely, the only way I could still use my talking laptop would be with something called a Braille display. This is a little keyboard with Braille on it that goes in front of your computer. When emails are received, the Braille lifts up to read it and the person feels it. I had already said that I didn't want to learn Braille again because I had a lot of other things to deal with, but people kept going on about it, telling me if I lost my hearing I needed to know it, but I didn't want to think about that. I went to a centre to feel a Braille display and left feeling even worse because it seemed impossible. Again I said I wasn't ready to learn it, but the Braille lessons were booked, so even though I wasn't happy about it, I agreed to give one lesson a go. But I never got there, as a week before the session, the following happened . . .

I coped with everything for as long as I could, but at the end of August 2008, I broke down. It was one of those moments when it all just comes out, and boy did it come out. I'd woken up in an OK kind of mood, then Mum told me that a test I'd had for a suspected infection had come back with inconclusive results, like the previous tests, and the problem didn't seem to be getting fixed. This put me in a bad mood. I started feeling panicky, and my heart began beating really fast. Then Mum came in my room and said, 'What's wrong with you?' and I just burst out crying. It then turned into a major panic attack where I struggled to breathe properly, I felt faint and weak, my hands and feet hurt and felt tingly, and I was sobbing.

I've always said I'm not as strong as people think,

and there's only so much I can take before I break. The last year and a half had become too much. From realising there was a problem, not being able to get anyone to listen, my hearing getting worse, then becoming virtually deaf, trying gadget after gadget which didn't help – it was just one disappointment after another and I'd had enough. I knew it was coming though. I'm surprised it took so long, to be honest. I'd been having little panic attacks for months beforehand, and I think it was because I didn't quite know how to handle what was going on and I was scared I'd lose the little bit of hearing I did have left.

After my 'moment', though, things got better. The meetings were cancelled, I stopped trying gadgets, and I was left to deal with it all in my own way, in my own time.

As harsh as it might sound, I can never forgive the people involved with what happened to my hearing – the ones I kept going back to but yet they wouldn't listen. When will people realise that I know my own body, and when I say something is wrong, something is wrong? Losing my hearing has been the hardest thing I've ever had to deal with, and I don't think I'll ever fully come to terms with it. It's just something I'm learning to cope with more. I just hope this can be another case where doctors and nurses can learn from their mistakes. Then hopefully someone else won't have to go through what I have.

Now, my hearing is kind of stable. Well I say hearing, but I haven't really got much of it. My left ear is completely deaf. My right ear has about 10–15 per cent hearing left, but it just lets me hear noise rather than voices. I feel lucky to have that bit of hearing though as it helps me judge situations. I can hear if someone comes into a room or if I'm in a busy or quiet place. The tumours from the start have caused tinnitus, so I always have banging, buzzing and other funny noises in my ears. This can be really annoying but it can't be helped. Sometimes it's worse than other days, especially if I'm tired, and it means I can't hear my talking laptop with the little bit of hearing in my right ear because it's filled with tinnitus sounds. The tumours have also badly affected my balance. I can't sit up any more without wobbling and when I try to walk I'm very wobbly on my feet. I'm having physiotherapy to try and make this a bit better.

After realising that, despite being pink, the hearing aids wouldn't help me, I continued to have meetings and tests on my ears for the following year to see what else could be done. One of these tests showed that the nerve in my left ear is damaged, but the cochlea still works. This is a good thing as it means I can now have a cochlea implant fitted which should help me hear better. I'm not sure how it is going to work as I haven't had it done yet but I will have an operation to have the cochlea fitted inside my skull with a magnet attached just behind my ear. You won't know it's there but the security at airports might! I will use a hearing aid, pink of course, which will go on my ear and pick up the magnet inside and start doing its stuff. It will take me many months to get used to. It won't give me perfect hearing again though. I'll be able to hear the tune and melody of music, but not the lyrics. I'll need to retrain my brain to recognise what sounds are, as everything will sound different. I'll need to keep repeating noises until I know what the sound is. For example, when the phone rings, Mum will have to keep saying, 'That's the phone', until I learn what that sound is, and I'll have to keep asking people to talk to me so that I can get used to their voice. I know it will be a very frustrating process, but if it helps me in some way to hear better, then it's worth it.

Causing confusion
...again

While I was having the radiotherapy for the acoustic neuromas, I went to Guy's Hospital in London to see Ros Ferner, the neurofibromatosis specialist I saw when I was eleven, when I was suspected to have neurofibromatosis type 1 (NF1). My type of cancer is connected with NF1, and I also have some of the other symptoms such as scoliosis (curvature of the spine) and café au lait birthmarks, but I didn't have enough of the classic symptoms so I wasn't diagnosed with NF1 and always had a question mark after it on my medical notes. Ros said that after seeing me in 2000, she then saw lots of other children who, like me, had a mosaic form of neurofibromatosis, so I started a trend!

I was referred to see Ros again because the acoustic neuromas are a sign of neurofibromatosis type 2 (NF2), which is much rarer than NF1. She still couldn't give me a diagnosis though. I had a genetics test done which was a blood test, and it took three months for the result. Ros also went over my notes again and asked for another biopsy to be done on my first tumour (which is still in a jar somewhere – how gross!). When we got the results of the genetics test, it was negative. Mum and I were shocked about that because we were convinced that it would be positive. It seemed too much of a coincidence for it to not be NF2. It then got us thinking, well what are the tumours then? No one knew what they were, so it was then decided after another several appointments with Ros and other NF specialists, that I will have the tumour in my left ear removed and biopsied as that is the only way of finding out what the tumours are. This will be done in early 2010, so hopefully then we might get some answers.

Tips If You're Feeling Stressed

These are some of the things that I do when I'm stressed, anxious or wound up, and they usually help me calm down and relax.

Touch something cold

This might sound a bit strange, but I find it really calms me. Often when I'm stressed, angry or wound up I feel hot, so it makes sense to cool down –

literally. It can be anything really, from holding a cold can of Coke or something metal, to eating an ice cube or ice cream. I focus on the coldness and imagine it taking over my body and de-stressing me.

Top 3 cold things:

1. A cold flannel. Hold it in your hands or on your forehead. It should help to really cool you down.

2. A cold drink. Preferably one in a can that's been in the fridge.

3. Something metal i.e. a radiator - but one that hasn't been on of course! - or the fridge. This may not always be made of metal, but it's bloomin' cold!

Breathe deeply

OK, you can look a bit like an idiot while you're doing this one, but it really does help, and it's one of my top tips. If you get really stressed or a situation gets too much, just stop, forget everything you're doing, and breathe. Do it from your lower stomach, and breathe slowly. In and out, in and out. Think, all is good in the world and I am not stressed. In and out, in and out. Think of cake, Tetley, cute little puppies, fairies and butterflies. In and out, in and out. And if all that fails then just scream and let it all out!

Top 3 things to focus on while breathing:

1. How stupid do I look? Very, but never mind.

2. Is this really helping? Yes, just keep focusing on it.

3. The lovely Lemar (or whoever floats your boat!).

Positive pain

I'm luckily strong enough to resist the temptation of getting into the world of self harm, but I can understand the release self-harmers get by hurting themselves. I've never self-harmed, but sometimes when I've been frustrated and having a major hissy fit, I've accidentally hurt myself, like banged my arm on the side, and it made me feel better. Instead, when I'm frustrated I create what I call 'positive pain'. By this I mean doing something that can hurt you, but you benefit from it. For example, waxing your legs or plucking your eyebrows. It can hurt like hell, but strangely it makes you feel good afterwards. Plus, you look much better too!

Top 3 things to cause 'positive pain':

1. Waxing your eyebrows. I much prefer this to plucking. The hair takes longer to grow back and waxing gets the job done quicker too!

2. Waxing your legs. Ouch - but super-smooth effect!

3. Doing a lot of sit-ups or some other kind of exercise. This should help you get your frustration out too and make you feel better.

F O U R

Needle Nightmare

I decided in the summer of 2007 that I couldn't handle my needle phobia any more, and I had to do something about it. It had got really bad, and I would have panic attacks and go pale, feel faint and sick before having a cannula put in my hand. I'd cry hysterically but also laugh at the same time because I felt so stupid. It was so dramatic and I could have won an Oscar for my performance sometimes, but I really, really couldn't help it. I can control all my other emotions and usually manage not to cry even if I feel like it, but when it comes to needles – I'm completely powerless.

Then, on a rare visit to my GP (I normally deal with specialists, so never go to my GP) I asked if anything could be done because it was really getting to me, and she suggested taking a Valium tablet to calm me down before I have a cannula put in. I took a low dose of Valium an hour before my next cannula, and it helped quite a lot. It calmed me down and I didn't feel as anxious or as panicky as usual. I still didn't like it, but I managed to hold back the tears, something that I couldn't do before.

At the time, I was being transferred from children's to adult services as I was eighteen, and was referred to the Pilgrims Hospice in Canterbury, which is the adult equivalent of Demelza House. Some of the services they offer are reflexology and massage treatments, and hypnotherapy. While having a meeting with someone from the Pilgrims Hospice, I explained about my phobia and asked if I could try hypnotherapy to see if that could help. I'd tried it twice before and it didn't work, but I wasn't prepared to deal with it then, whereas now I was determined to overcome the phobia.

The day I saw the hypnotherapist, Nanette, was one of the most emotional days of my life, but a real breakthrough. I spent practically the whole ninety-minute session hysterical. I don't quite know what happened to me, but it all just came out! I kind of shocked myself as I had gone prepared not to react like that, and I hadn't realised just how bad my phobia was. It didn't take long for us to realise that my fear isn't of the actual needle, but of the 'process' involved with it. I'm not a wimp and it's not the pain I'm scared of, it's everything else involved with it. From travelling to the hospital knowing what's going to happen, waiting in the ward, preparing the cannula, opening the packets etc. My problem is anxiety, so it's the build-up to it happening that I can't handle.

We began hypnotherapy by learning breathing techniques. When I'm having a cannula put in I have panic attacks and my breaths are quick and from my chest. Nannette taught me to take long deep breaths from my lower stomach, and to focus on that rather than what's going on. We did that for around thirty minutes, then she got me to talk through the needle process. I talked through it twice and was fine, then the third time I felt myself go a bit wobbly, so we went back to deep breathing. Nanette asked me to imagine someone I love and I said my dogs. She asked their names and I said, 'Molly and Daizy.' She told me to imagine cuddling

Molly, which I did and I felt relaxed again. Then she said, 'Now, while you're still cuddling Molly, I'm going to bring a needle towards you.' Well, that's when the crying started and it never really stopped. I completely lost it. When Nanette asked why I was upset, I wailed, 'Because Molly's here!' Obviously she wasn't. It sounds funny now, but I was distraught at the time. Just the thought of the thing I hate most in the world, and that I know is painful, being anywhere near my dogs, who are the things I love most in the world, was too much to handle.

I hadn't really thought about my phobia before, because I didn't want to, but speaking about it really helped me understand my fear. If someone has a fear of heights or spiders, they just have to avoid them. I can't avoid needles because I have to keep having them stuck in me. I also said something without thinking, but once I'd said it everything made total sense. It was that I can't deal with the fear and move on and put it in the past because needles are my future, and I'm always going to have to deal with them.

Mum was in the room with me but wasn't allowed to do or say anything. I'd calmed down a bit by the end of the session, and I was laughing at how stupid I was by the time we got to the car. Then

Mum explained Nanette didn't have a needle in the room like I thought. It was all to see my reaction. I know that sounds mean, but it had to be done so that she could see my true reaction. If I had known there wasn't a needle near me I would have put my front on as usual and pretended I was OK.

We decided that hypnotherapy wouldn't work, but counselling would, so that was me then 'in therapy'. My next session with Nanette was much better and there were no tears. The first session got it out of my system, and I was then ready to start taking control and dealing with my phobia. I haven't always had a fear of needles. I never *liked* having them stuck in me, but I wasn't scared of them. I decided to try and work out when the change happened, and one day it clicked. It was during my three-month stay in hospital after my brain haemorrhage, and I had to have a blood test. I hadn't had the numbing cream on my hand and I didn't want it done. The doctor, who will remain nameless, tried four times to get the needle in my vein properly and I was getting really upset. I got to the stage where I was screaming and he was getting really annoyed with me and telling me to be quiet. Eventually he walked off in a stress and his boss had to come and do it. I was scared from then on that all my needle experiences would be like that and I think that's where the change happened, and over the years the phobia just got worse and more intense.

It got to the point where it was making me miserable, and I was fed up of being scared and not in control, so that's when I knew I needed to do something. The Valium helped to control my subconscious, which I couldn't, and I worked on my breathing while I was having a blood test or cannula done. The combination seemed to work. I still felt panicky, but the tears stopped. I always wanted to cry afterwards but it was only from relief. For the first year it was a bit hit or miss, though. Sometimes I was absolutely fine and as cool as a cucumber about it, and other times I would just break down. Now I have more good days than bad with needles. I don't cry, and don't really get panicky any more. Well, apart from if it goes wrong the first try, and the second – I can't help but lose it by the third attempt! But it's something I'm very glad I faced up to. It's made life a lot easier and less stressful too – for the doctors as well as me!

I'm not over my fear, I never will be, I've just learnt how to deal with it better.

More Tips If You're Feeling Stressed

Random ranting!

I enjoy nothing more than having a good old rant. Often about very random things. I've normally been feeling stressed for a while, and it will take something really stupid, like finding out there's no nice 'n' spicy Nik Naks left, to make me 'go off on one', and that's why my rants are random! To be honest, it doesn't take much to wind me up – it's easily done, so I often have a rant about things. It really helps me get my frustration out! It doesn't always solve the problem, but it makes me feel better anyway, so I'd definitely recommend it. So go on, strop 'til you drop!

If you can't rant out loud, write it down. You can probably say a lot more of what you want to if you do it that way. Then, a month or two later, read it back. You'll probably find it funny that you were so wound up about something, and it might help put things into perspective. Besides, you've probably got bigger problems to worry about by then anyway.

I once read a little poem which I remind myself of whenever I think a situation can't get any worse, and it makes me realise that's life, and puts things into perspective again. It's . . . 'friends you'll make and hearts will break, and tears will always fall, the world is turning and you are learning – that's what matters most of all'.

Top 3 things to rant about:

1. People - the main reason for my ranting. Even if they don't mean to wind me up, it still happens!

2. Life. When things go wrong or don't go the way I planned, it stresses me out and often results in a rant.

3. Who ate the last chocolate doughnut? Major rant required then, but the culprit is usually my brother Lee ...

Exercise

It can be hard work exercising, but there are a lot of benefits to doing a load of press-ups or running for a long time. Your arms and legs will ache a lot afterwards, but it's a known fact that exercise makes you feel good. It's prescribed by doctors, you know! It can also come under the 'positive pain' category as your body aches a lot if you do a good work-out.

I feel great whenever I've finished a gym session or been in the hydrotherapy pool. Before I go, I always think to myself, 'I really can't be bothered,' but I know that I always feel great afterwards and I'm glad I went, so I make sure I keep going.

Top 3 ways to exercise:

1. Walking. I may be disabled, but it doesn't mean I can't walk. I use parallel bars at the gym where I hold on to a long bar either side of me, and walk along the inside of them and keep moving my hands along the bar as I walk. I also have a very sexy zimmer frame and 'granny trolley', which comes complete with a little seat and a basket on the front. I use these frames in the house when I want to walk from my bedroom to the living room.

2. Doing sit-ups and press-ups. I like exercises which I can do on my own. With the walking, I always need someone there to support me in case I fall over, but sit-ups, press-ups, leg lifts etc. I can do on my own when I'm just lying in bed, so I can do those whenever I want and don't need to wait for someone to help me.

3. Swimming. OK, technically I don't like swimming as I have a slight fear of water

and avoid it as much as possible, but I love being in the hydrotherapy pool. This is a small swimming pool where people can do exercises as it's much easier doing them in water than it is on dry land. The water tends to only go up to your shoulder which is great because it means it's not near my face which is the part I don't like. It's why I refuse to swim on my front no matter how much my physiotherapist tries to make me!

Pillow punching

Go on, give it a good whack! Whatever's wound you up, get it all out by punching a pillow. If a person has annoyed you, imagine it's them. I don't condone violence, so please don't punch the person, the pillow will do. If you don't feel better afterwards, at least you've built your muscles up a bit!

Top 3 things to think about while punching the pillow:

1. Violence is not the answer. Apart from right now.

2. My muscles must be bulging by now.

3. Oops, there fly the feathers . . . cough.

N.B. feather pillows not recommended. You might not thank me for turning your room into a feather factory, and neither will your parents.

F   I   V   E

Target Met and New One Set

In June 2008 I finally did it – I reached my £30,000 fund-raising target for the Silver Lining Appeal, a campaign launched in 2004 by King's College Hospital to buy new specialist equipment for the children's ward. I was an ambassador for the appeal and set my target in early 2006 to fund a neuro-rehabilatation room.

On 11th June I won 'Britain's Most Inspiring Fundraiser', an award launched that year by the charity search engine, everyclick.com, in memory of the famous fund-raiser, Jane Tomlinson. There were 600 entries for the competition from across the UK, and I found out I'd made the top ten. I was invited to an award ceremony in London along with the nine other finalists.

On the afternoon of the award ceremony, I had a photo-shoot at the office of everyclick.com, where I was having photos taken by a *Sun* newspaper photographer because they were sponsoring the event.

Mum and I went back to our hotel after the photo-shoot to get ready, and then headed to Warner Brothers where the award ceremony was taking place. Paul from the Silver Lining Appeal was there too, which was lovely. They showed footage of each of the finalists, then Mike Tomlinson, the husband of Jane, gave a short speech. Mum had been signing on my hand all the way through and was signing that he was about to announce the winner, but before she could finish the sentence, Mike had announced it was me! Mum kept touching my little finger, which is the letter U in the deafblind sign language, but I didn't believe her. Then I realised it really was me and I was absolutely gobsmacked. I really, really, really wasn't expecting to win. I was just so pleased already to have made the top ten, so I was absolutely over the moon that I won! Mum couldn't spell properly on my hand for ages afterwards because she was so excited!

I now know that the other finalists didn't have their photos taken earlier with the *Sun*, like I'd been told. It was just me! I'd also given an email interview with the *Sun*, which I thought the other finalists had done too, but it was just me again. It all seems obvious now, but I honestly didn't have a clue at the time, or twig that I was the winner, so it made the surprise all the more amazing.

Mike Tomlinson presented me with a giant cheque. The prize was £20,000 for my chosen charity, Silver Lining. As I had already raised over £21,000, it meant, I'D REACHED MY TARGET!! So it was a double celebration for me on the night!

I officially finished my fund-raising for the Silver Lining Appeal on 6th July 2008 when I did a 100ft sponsored abseil down the side of King's College Hospital in the middle of London! I had already signed up for it before I'd reached my target, so I then decided to use the abseil as my final event. It was a brilliant way to end my fund-raising for King's College Hospital, by abseiling down it!

We arrived at the hospital at lunch-time, and it was only then that it dawned on me what I was doing! I met Matt, the guy I was doing the abseil with, and he explained everything. I then had a safety harness attached round my waist and thighs, plus a yellow hard hat, so I felt highly unattractive. We headed for the roof and I started to get a bit anxious, but only because I had absolutely no idea how I was actually going to do it. Even though it had been explained to me, I just couldn't imagine it in my head.

Once I was on the roof, I stood up with help from Mum and Matt, then sat on the floor. There I forgot about my nerves because I was concentrating on what I was doing. I had my legs dangling over the edge, where there was a bar in front of me which I had to slide under, then stand up again on a ledge on the outside of the building. I had to ask several times if they were sure there was a ledge below me before I stood up because I was convinced it was just air and the long drop to the ground beneath me! It was difficult to be told what to do as I had thick gloves on, so couldn't feel Mum doing the deafblind sign language, and it was windy that high up in the sky so I couldn't hear in my good ear. When I was standing on the ledge (which luckily did exist!), I had to turn around so that my back was to the crowd below and kneel down. But

I couldn't actually bend my right knee because it was too close to the wall and I haven't got much strength in my leg to move it back, so I did start to panic slightly. At last I managed to move my leg and knelt down, then lay on my stomach with my legs dangling over the edge; this time it was the actual 'edge', where the only thing below me was a lot of sky and the ground! Oh, and Matt of course! I was still holding on to the bar in front of me and refused to let go at first. I had to put all of my trust

in the harness, that it would catch me when I let go, but finally I did! The split second between letting go and the harness catching me was the scary part. The rest was just brilliant!

The only words I said on the way down were 'Oh my God' and 'Argh'. It hurt my back quite a lot as the only thing supporting it was the belt round my waist, and my legs were just dangling. It took about two minutes to abseil down the building. I had to hold on to the safety rope with my right hand at all times, and with my left hand I held on to the front of the harness. Matt lowered us down slowly, but every now and again he would do it quite fast and that was the best part! Then I landed safely on the ground. I stamped my foot a couple of times to make sure it was safe! I got a round of applause as I had an audience of about a hundred people. It was lots of doctors, nurses and staff from the hospital who knew I was abseiling at that time so came out to watch.

Lee also did the abseil that day. He wasn't meant to, but he came with us and when he saw what people were doing, he wanted to join in, and they kindly said he could. If I thought I looked bad in a harness and hard hat, you should have seen Lee!

It was a fun day despite the rain, and a great way

to celebrate the end of my fund-raising for King's. The abseil raised £1,500 in sponsorship money, so I was really pleased with that. It brought my full total raised for the Silver Lining Appeal to . . . drumroll please . . . £43,629.38! So I think it's fair to say I smashed my original £30,000 target!

Nicole's Sweet

In January 2010, Nicole's Sweet was officially opened on the children's ward at King's College Hospital. It's a two-bed neuro-rehabilitation suite for children recovering from the severest of brain and spinal injuries, and like me, it's totally unique in the NHS! Often, the children using this room will have to learn everything again, from walking and talking, to moving and eating, as their injuries are so severe. The equipment in the room is the best though, so these children now have a better chance of recovering as neuro-rehabilitation is essential to a good recovery. The children will receive multidisciplinary care while in the room, including physiotherapy, occupational therapy, speech and language therapy, visits from a play specialist, along with dietician, medical and nursing care. I could have benefited from a room like this while I was on the children's ward for three months after my brain haemorrhage, which is why I wanted to raise the money to have the room there now.

The room is called 'Nicole's Sweet', with the apostrophe in Nicole's as a sweet shape. That sign is on the outside of the room and is the only thing that's pink. I wasn't allowed any more pink than that! Inside the room there are pictures of piles of brightly coloured sweets above each bed. The sweet theme was my idea as I love sweets and thought it was good for any age, so hopefully whether a two-year-old or sixteen-year-old is using the room, they'll like it. I also wanted it to be brightly coloured to make the room more cheerful for the children in there.

The room has two electric beds that can be moved into the sitting position, a hoist in the ceiling above each bed to lift children in and out, a flat-screen TV, PlayStation 3 and a laptop at each bed, and a remote control system that children with very limited mobility can use to operate the TV, music system, curtains etc., all by the touch of a button. There's also two parents' beds so that they can stay with their children, but best of all – there's two funky fish tanks on the walls! I'm so glad that this room is now available, and I hope it makes a big difference to the children who use it.

Nicole's new fund

After winning such an important title as 'Britain's most inspiring fundraiser', there was no way I was going to give up fund-raising now that I'd reached one target – I had a reputation to keep up after all! I decided to stop fund-raising for King's College Hospital and move on to support another charity. I knew immediately the charity I wanted to fund-raise for next and I then set myself a new target – to raise £50,000 for Teenage Cancer Trust (TCT), a charity devoted to improving the lives of teenagers and young adults with cancer. Their main aim is to build special state-of-the-art units in NHS hospitals for 13–24-year-olds going through treatment for cancer, and of course, it's a charity very, very close to my heart.

Just before I reached my £30,000 target for the Silver Lining Appeal, Teenage Cancer Trust announced that they were going to build one of their specialist units at the Royal Marsden Hospital in Sutton, Surrey, where I've had my cancer treatment since I was eleven years old, so that's why I knew straight away that this was the next charity I wanted to fund-raise for. I set up 'Nicole's

Fund' with TCT so that the money I raise goes specifically to the Royal Marsden Hospital to help build the new unit. Each unit costs over £2 million, so I want to do as much as possible to help.

I doubled my target after a while to £100,000, as this is how much it costs to fully equip one patient's bedroom on a TCT unit. This includes an electric bed, plasma screen TV, laptop with internet access, games console, music system, en-suite bathroom and lots more. Basically the room is filled with everything a teenager would want, all so their experience of going through treatment for cancer is the best it can possibly be.

Nicole's Fund was officially launched on 15th April 2009 – at Number 11 Downing Street! It was hosted by the Chancellor's wife, Maggie Darling, and I had over a hundred special guests. There were speeches from Professor Tim Eden, who is funded by Teenage Cancer Trust (and is the only professor of teenage and young adult cancer in the UK) and Marc Wood (a trustee for TCT, he had cancer when he was seventeen years old and has won several gold medals in the Paralympics). I also gave a speech at the end, which was over twenty minutes long. We had lots of cakes and biscuits, including a giant cake which had been specially made, and had white icing on it with lots of strawberries and raspberries on it (so it looked quite pink), and 'Nicole's Fund' written in chocolate. It was brilliant – and it served all of the hundred guests! I received a special message from Princess Beatrice, whom I had met a few weeks earlier, and Prince Harry sent me this lovely message of support which is in the brochure for the appeal.

The launch party went really well and it was a lovely way to officially launch my fund. I left with lots of new mad ideas of how to raise money!

The first big fund-raising event I organised for my fund was a chocolate ball on 12th September 2009. It was held at the Pavilion in Broadstairs, Kent, and the theme, of course, was chocolate! It took me about a year to organise and I had everything just the way I wanted it – majorly pink!

I arrived at the venue in a white limo covered in pink bows, and was met by Andy who filmed the night to make into a DVD. We had a marquee which was covered on the inside with white silk drapes, and a gold chandelier hung from the ceiling! The hall was decorated with lots of pink balloons including a balloon arch above the stage and tall stands covered in balloons. The tablecloths

When I first met Nicole Dryburgh last October, she casually mentioned to me that she had just abseiled down the side of King's College Hospital. How very typical of her! That achievement is just an instance in the life of an incredibly brave, fun-loving and, frankly, awe-inspiring person.

I was, therefore, not in the least surprised to hear that Nicole has now set herself a new challenge: to raise £100,000 for the Teenage Cancer Trust's new unit at The Royal Marsden Hospital in Sutton. I know that Nicole will achieve this remarkable goal; her determination and resolve to help others is simply phenomenal.

It is a huge privilege for me to wish Nicole the very best of luck with the success of her Fund, and I look forward to hearing about the innovative and challenging ways in which she will achieve this.

Harry

were white with a pink shimmery overlay on top; the napkins were pink; there were white silky covers on the chairs with big pink bows on them; and we had pink wineglass charms on the glasses. In the middle of the tables were either tall vases of flowers or glass vases filled with marshmallows and Maltesers with a pink candle in the middle! I had hired two chocolate fountains – one milk chocolate fountain and one pink chocolate fountain! I'd also arranged for special pink chocolates to be made with 'Nicole's Fund' written in milk chocolate on them, as well as some mini chocolate Jengas!

The ball started with a drinks reception in the marquee where guests arrived along the hot pink carpet! It was followed by a performance from Flava, a brilliant dance crew who made the semi-finals of *Britain's Got Talent* in 2008. We then sat down for a three-course meal and Flava performed again in between each course. After the meal, I gave a speech, then showed a special DVD that I'd had made for the night. When I relapsed from my cancer when I was seventeen, I filmed my journey through chemotherapy so that I could show what it's really like. My friend Nick kindly edited the footage into a ten-minute DVD, which we showed on the night and which made everyone cry!

The Way I see it launch party, with Mum and Lee.

Book signing, with my 'stamp' in Waterstone's.

Prince Charming – at Clarence House with Prince Harry.

Nicole's Fund launch party, hosted by Maggie Darling at 11 Downing Street.

Charity Abseil – down the side of King's College Hospital, raising £1,500 for the Silver Lining Appeal.

Only 100ft until the ground ...

Safe and sound – I did it

NICOLE'S FUND

Chocolate Ball –
Dancing, Charity
and Chocolate.

The night raised £9,000 for Nicole's Fund.

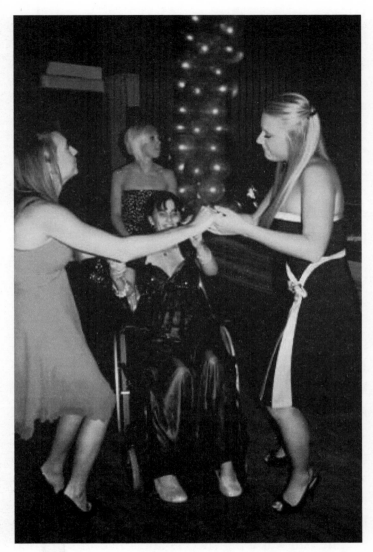

Nicole dancing with The Girls at the Chocolate Ball

We then had an auction of original artwork done by some of Hachette Children's Books' best illustrators. The chocolate fountains were started after that, along with the 'tree of wishes'. This was a lovely white tree covered in twinkly fairy lights. Silver, baby blue and baby pink (the colour theme of the ball) envelopes were pegged on to it, and each had a piece of paper inside with a prize written on it. Guests chose an envelope after making a donation and won whatever was written on the paper inside.

Then there was a fab performance from a Kent stage school who had lots of sparkly dancers and a great singer. After that it was time for the main auction. We had some amazing prizes donated, including a T-shirt worn and signed by Orlando Bloom, two lovely dresses donated by Holly Willoughby and a voucher for a pair of custom-made Jimmy Choos! The real party started around 11 p.m. with a live band who played lots of rock music, and the night finished in the small hours with a great DJ. Actually, the night finished with me doing the conga! Practically the whole place joined in!

The ball was a big success and I had lots of good feedback, so I'm hoping to make it an annual event.

The chocolate ball raised over £9,000, which made a big difference to my fund.

I'm very passionate about having this fund with Teenage Cancer Trust. It's such an amazing charity, and since becoming involved with them, I've found out just how big an issue teenage cancer is and it's made me even more determined to raise money and awareness for TCT.

Some of the facts of teenage cancer really shock and scare me, such as, one in every 312 boys, and one in every 361 girls gets cancer by the age of twenty, and there are now more teenagers than children living with cancer. Young people contract some of the rarest and most aggressive types of cancer and the survival rate falls well below that of other ages.

The figure that stands out most for me though is that, every single day in the UK, six teenagers and young adults are diagnosed with cancer. That's six today, six tomorrow, six the day after and the day after that. It's over two thousand young people a year. When we all go to sleep tonight, six young people's lives have been turned upside down. I know how that feels, and it's the worst feeling ever.

That's the thought I have all the time now, and it's what spurs me on and makes me so passionate about the charity. I was never lucky enough to be treated on a Teenage Cancer Trust unit, so I want to do what I can to make other young people's experience of cancer better than mine.

Fantastic fund-raising

As you can probably tell, fund-raising is one of my favourite things to do. I'm constantly thinking of ideas and organising fund-raising events – I think I'm actually addicted to it, along with Tetley tea, of course! But it's a good addiction to have so I'm not ashamed to admit it!

I first started fund-raising in 2003, when I was fourteen. I donated a giant teddy bear to my school which they raffled for CLIC (Cancer and Leukaemia in Children), and it raised almost £500, and from then on, I was hooked. I then started to organise fund-raising events to help the charities that had supported me in my recovery after my brain haemorrhage, and the first event I organised was a coffee morning at my friend's house in aid of two charities, the Silver Lining Appeal and RDA (Riding for the Disabled Association). The event included a raffle, bring and buy, crafts, cakes and, of course, tea and coffee. It raised £420.15, which I was really surprised by. My goal had been to raise £60, which is the amount it costs to shoe a horse at RDA, then anything else I raised I was going to give to the Silver Lining Appeal, so you can imagine how chuffed I was, and a few months later I held my second coffee morning at another friend's house which raised over £470 for Demelza House children's hospice in Kent.

I've organised a lot of different fund-raising events over the years, including concerts, coffee mornings, an Easter fair at school for children with learning and physical disabilities, sponsored silences (one for 36 hours – not to be repeated!), and a seven-mile sponsored walk along the seafront with friends and family, where I walked the last thirty steps with the help of Mum and my physiotherapist.

My tips on starting fund-raising would first of all be, find a charity to support, whose work you think is *really* important. There are thousands and thousands out there to choose from so it won't be difficult to find one that suits you. Then decide roughly how much you'd like to raise as this will determine what sort of event you need to do, and how much effort you'll need to put in.

If you only want to raise a small amount, then I'd recommend doing a sponsored event, and from my experience, the more difficult or random the thing is that you want to do, the more money you raise. My 36-hour sponsored silence raised £450, whereas my sponsored abseil raised £1,500. Try to get other people involved and to do the event with you; you'll obviously raise more money that way, and it'll be more fun too!

If, however, you want to raise a big amount you need to plan a big event. This is more hard work, but it'll be totally worth it when you're counting the money that you've raised, and hand the cheque over to the charity, so bear that in mind if you get stressed with the organising. If there's no stress involved with a big event then there's something wrong! In order to organise a really good event, I'd recommend planning it as much in advance as possible. That way you have longer to get it right and not rush it.

Fund-raising can be great fun – *fun* is in the word – and whatever you raise, it's always more than you started out with (providing it went well, of course), and it'll be helping a good cause, so why not give it a go . . .

Tips for Fund-raising

Sponsored events

You can get sponsored for doing pretty much anything these days, from a sponsored silence, walk, run, swim, head shave, abseil, bungee jump or sky dive, to more unusual things such as giving up cheese for a month (I swear a guy did this once) and going to work dressed as Shrek (I don't think that's been done before – but what a good idea!).

Five easy steps to organising a sponsored event:

1. Contact the charity you're going to be fund-raising for and let them know about your event. They can send you information and sponsorship forms for you to collect sponsorship from family and friends.

2. This is optional, but I'd recommend it. Set up a Justgiving page at www.justgiving.com, which is a brilliant service which lets you fundraise online free of charge. You can set up your own page, add a personal message and photo, and watch your fund-raising total growing. I've had a couple of Justgiving pages, and they're really useful to raise money online. The money goes directly to the charity.

3. Ask friends, family, workmates etc. to sponsor you for your event, either on your sponsorship form or by giving them the address of your Justgiving page. Also try contacting your local paper to see if they

would write an article about it and help spread the word.

4. Do your event – and have fun with it! If what you're doing isn't very nice, like bathing in baked beans, just keep reminding yourself why you're doing it, and that should help you through it.

5. Collect your sponsorship money and send it off to the charity. Then sit back and know that you just helped make a difference. It couldn't be any easier!

Organising a big event

Well first of all, and I know this probably seems obvious, but you have to decide on what type of event you want to organise. That will help you know what sort of venue you need, which is always the first thing you need to sort out. For coffee morning type events I'd recommend someone's house, or a church hall. For bigger events such as a ball, school halls or a hotel are ideal. Try and get a few friends on board to help you organise the event. Give everyone different jobs to do as this will make it easier and quicker to arrange the event. For example, have someone in charge of the decorations, someone else doing the food, another sorting out the promotion for the event etc. It's all about teamwork. I have a committee set up for Nicole's Fund with friends and supporters. We meet regularly to discuss events and ways to keep the money coming in. It's a good way to keep the fund moving forward.

Five easy steps to organising a successful event:

1. Find a venue and book a date for your event.

2. Get a group of people together to help. Each take on a different responsibility. You might want to have meetings every now and again to make sure plans are going well.

3. Contact businesses and shops to see if they will sponsor your event or donate a raffle/auction prize. By having your event sponsored, it means whatever costs you've

had in organising the event are paid for by the sponsor, and you don't have to take the money out of what's been raised. Therefore, the charity gets every single penny.

4. Once everything's organised, promote it and sell the tickets.

5. Have your event and then count the money!

S I X

Time For Tick Off

I want to:

Have hair down to my bra strap   ☐

Be in an advert   ☐

Be in *OK!* magazine   ☐

Be a millionaire   ☐

Wobble on the cobbles at Coronation   ☐
Street

Go sky-diving ☐

Do an abseil ☐

Walk in heels ☐

Go to New York ☐

Have my own documentary ☐

Publish a book ☐

Meet Prince Harry ☐

2008 was my year to start ticking the things off of 'my list', and boy did I have fun doing it!

It started at the beginning of the year, on 10th January, when I had my book launch.

I still can't actually believe that *The Way I See It* was published. I mean I was always determined that it would be, and I wouldn't have stopped trying until it was, but I never imagined it would be like it is now – with pink pages!

When I first started writing it at the age of fifteen, I never realised how much work actually goes into publishing a book. I honestly thought you

Nicole with The Girls at the book launch

just wrote a book and got it published. It didn't
occur to me that you actually needed someone to
agree to publish it, which now seems really obvious,
but at fifteen I was just a little bit naive! So I was a
little bit shocked when I found out how many
people are involved in the publishing process:
editors, cover designers, publicists, marketing
people etc. I loved finding out how it all happened,
and pretty soon – I had my book in my hands!

The book launch party was held at the

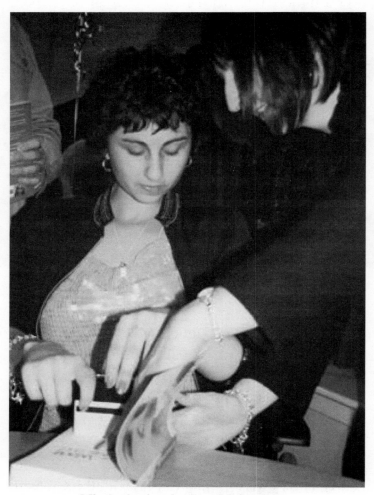

Nicole signing books with her stamp

Horsebridge centre in Whitstable, and there were over a hundred guests. I had invited all the people who I felt had supported me over the years and stood by me, and I wanted to thank them for it. There was quite a mix of people from family, friends, doctors, nurses, media, photographers and even the Lord Mayor! The hall was decorated brilliantly pink. There were pink balloons, little heart-shape chocolates in pink foil, big posters of my book and lots more. The food was great, and there was a big chocolate cake, but best of all, there were little square fairy cakes in silver cases, with pink sparkly icing, and on each one was a letter so that they together they spelled out 'The Way I See It' – absolutely brilliant and one of my favourite parts of the night, along with signing my book for everyone. There was a massive queue, but it wasn't too much hard work as I had a special stamp to sign the books with. I'd signed a piece of paper which Hodder, my publishers, had made into a stamp so that it's easier for me to sign my books for people. I have one stamp in black ink, and another in a pinky/purple colour.

My books were sold on the night for £5 each, with the proceeds going towards my £30,000 target for the Silver Lining Appeal. Hodder matched

what was raised, and rounded it up to make the total £2,000. I was presented with a giant cheque, and it made the night even more special.

And so that was me, a published author, and still only eighteen! Not bad huh?!

The next goal I ticked off my list, was to have hair down to my bra strap. My friend, Gilly, organised for me to have hair extensions fitted. When I was talking to Gilly one day about my list, and about some of the things on it, I said that because I've twice lost my hair through chemo, I'd love to have the feeling of long curly mermaid-like hair floating down my back. The next day she called to say she had arranged for her friend to fit hair extensions for me for free, but that we had to pay £400 for the hair. Gilly thought we could ask forty people to donate £10 each towards it, and that night she went out with her friends and raised £200! And over the next couple of weeks she managed to get the rest of the money. I only managed to raise £20 because I found it difficult asking people for money for myself, and not for charity, so luckily Gilly was brilliant at it.

I had the extensions fitted on 26th June at a salon in Herne Bay called Infusion. It took over four hours as there were 275 extensions to fit. My hair felt so big afterwards! The extensions were real hair and were a perfect match. It was exactly the same colour and had the same kind of curls as my real hair so no one could tell that they were extensions. It was great being able to tie my hair up in different styles. I got more compliments about it than ever. As my own hair grew over the months, the extensions moved further down my back, so in the end my hair did grow past my bra strap!

I had the extensions taken out after five months. Quite a few of them had already fallen out, so it was definitely time. I was sad to see them go, but also pleased to have my own hair back and that it was really long even without the extensions in!

Shop 'til you drop!

The day after I did my 100ft abseil, Mum, Lee and I jetted off to New York for ten days! This was all arranged by the Rotary Club, after I won a Rotary Young Citizen Award in April 2008. I went to an award ceremony in Blackpool to receive it along with the four other winners. The ceremony was filmed live by BBC News 24, and I was asked a few questions when I received my award, and one of them was about my wish list. I mentioned some of the things on it, one of which was to go shopping in New York, and afterwards, Tony from the Rotary Club of Redbridge offered to arrange my dream trip.

There was quite a lot to sort out beforehand, but on Monday 7th July we were on our way to New York! We arrived at Heathrow airport at about 11.30 a.m., where I was filmed by the BBC who had been making a documentary about me since I had won the award. It was then time for my anti-clotting injection, which I had to have just as a precaution for the long flight. I felt it go in, but I was very good about it! I was in quite a bit of pain anyway after the abseil. I hadn't realised just how much hard work it had been, but I was beginning to feel the effects. I didn't care though as I was off to NYC!

Our flights had been kindly donated by British Airways, and we flew business class which was very posh! We were allowed to relax in the first class area before our flight, which was good. I lay on a couch as my back was hurting, and fell asleep! Honestly, you can't take me anywhere! Plus, on the sofa next to me was a Formula 1 racing driver who was also on our flight! Take-off was a bit delayed due to bad weather, so we didn't leave until 4.30 p.m. The flight was over seven hours long, but it wasn't too bad because we were in really comfy seats that reclined so that you could go to sleep. That really helped my back as I wouldn't have been able to sit for seven hours without being in a lot of pain.

It was quite confusing when we arrived in New York, because to us it was then 1 a.m. Tuesday, but in America it was 8 p.m. Monday! The security at the airport was very, very tight. I even had my fingerprints taken! We were met by Taylor, a Rotarian who organised our days out while we were there. The heat was so strong when we got outside the airport. It was so hot that I could have got a suntan after about five minutes, which I found so

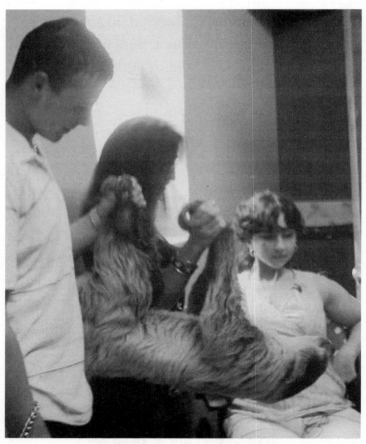

Nicole meets Frankie the sloth

strange because in my head it was 1 a.m.! We were then taken to our hotel, which was in Time's Square in Manhattan. Mum and I shared a room, and Lee got his own which even had a living room! These had also been donated, by the Time Hotel. We went straight to bed when we got to the hotel as it was now 3.30 a.m. to us, and we had now been up for almost twenty-four hours.

On Tuesday (officially our first day in New York), we went to Taylor's Rotary Club for lunch, where I also gave a small speech. It gave me a chance to thank everyone there who had helped organise my trip. Afterwards we went to the Bronx Zoo which was amazing! I was allowed to feed and hold a lot of the animals, which I loved. First I fed some goats, which slobbered all over my hands, but that was nothing compared to the sheep! I had lots of food poured into my hand and they just gobbled it up. My hand was covered in slime, and poor Mum had to touch it to sign on my hand. It was quite funny though, even if she didn't think so! I then fed another animal, but I didn't know what it was at first because I couldn't hear Mum, and she was refusing to sign on my hand while it was still slimy, but I soon found out it was a cow, which I was very impressed with! It was a cute little Friesian cow with horns, and after that I fed a llama! I then sat on a haystack and held a chicken and a guinea pig, you know, as you do. Then came the best part. I touched a sloth, which was very strange. She was called Frankie and hangs upside down all the time, and once a week she comes down to go to the toilet, then hangs upside down again! Classy girl! She had short hair on her stomach, and quite long hair on her back, plus very long nails. She desperately needed a manicure! After that I held an armadillo. Yes, an actual armadillo! It was curled up into a small ball and was quite hard. I wanted to knock on it to see how hard, but I thought it was best not to! Then I held a gorgeous big-eared fox, a tiny tortoise which fitted in my hand (and very nearly my pocket!) and a snake! I held the snake for about five minutes, which I loved. It was a very friendly snake and gave my hand a kiss! How polite! The visit was filmed by the BBC for my documentary, and it was my favourite day out while we were there.

On Wednesday we went to the Statue of Liberty. Security was really tight and we were checked going on and off the ferry and again on the island before we got anywhere near the statue. Normally I don't like boats as I have a slight fear of water, but the ferry ride was lovely because we sat on the top deck with the sun on us while eating hot dogs! I got to feel the statue, including her giant nose and toes! Only thing was, I didn't realise it was the body of the Statue of Liberty. I'd got a bit confused as I was sure our schedule for that day said we were going to the Empire State Building, so that's where I thought we were and that the nose and toes belonged to King Kong! It wasn't until we were back at our hotel, when Mum gave me a pink bag and T-shirt with a glittery picture of the statue on it, that she'd bought me, that I said, 'Why is there a picture of the Statue of Liberty on it if we went to see King Kong?' She then explained where we had actually been all day. Oh deary me!

We got the ferry again on Thursday to Staten Island to have lunch at Staten Island Rotary Club. Time again for a small speech, thank you and question and answer session from the people there, which mostly starts with, 'What is your mother doing on your hand?' It was the deafblind sign language!

On Friday we went to the New York Botanical Gardens. We travelled round the gardens on a golf buggy and stopped at a few of Henry Moore's sculptures, and I was allowed to feel them, which is a real honour. Then we went for a walk around the children's garden, which was lovely because the sun was really hot and I was starting to get a proper tan! We picked some of the things from the garden, like lettuce and chives, which at the end of our walk they made into a salad for us! We came back to the hotel after that and that's when we finally found the shops! It turned out we had been going the wrong way for four days and that's why we couldn't find the good shops! I bought a few things, and once I had a shopping bag in my hands I was able to officially tick off another goal on my list – to go shopping in New York, and it was great!

On Saturday and Sunday I did some major shopping. We had lost the first four days due to not being able to find the shops, so I had a lot to catch up on! The shops were near to our hotel, so every couple of hours I could go back for a lie-down and drop off the bags, then go back out again to do more shopping! The shops were open until really late at night, which was brilliant because we could visit places during the day and go shopping at night!

We went to Fraunces Tavern museum on Monday. It was built in 1719 and has a lot of history attached to it. George Washington had lunch there once, and now so did we! We then had a tour of the museum where I was allowed to touch some of the things, including a sword that belonged to General George Clinton (ancestor of President Clinton).

On Tuesday we went to the Metropolitan Museum of Art where I was again allowed to go behind the scenes and feel some of the artefacts, all of which had been arranged by the local congressman. We visited the Egyptians exhibition, and I felt a 3,000-year-old coffin. Some of the things were so big that I had to actually stand up to be able to feel them properly. They even stopped building work on a temple for half an hour so that I was able to hear! The BBC filmed this too, and afterwards we walked to Central Park, which was nearby, for me to do a final interview.

It was lovely in the park as the grass had just been cut so it smelt nice, and the sun was really hot, so it was a perfect end to our holiday. I got a a big ice lolly, which was basically a frozen slush puppy. It was great though it made my mouth blue for the interview! That night was our last night out.

Some of my favourite parts of the holiday were going out to eat, especially breakfast at a café that did lovely pancakes and maple syrup, and to a restaurant that did the best pizza ever. I don't know what it was about New York, but it made me obsessed with food! I normally eat hardly anything, and get full up really easily, but I just wanted to keep eating while we were in NYC!

Wednesday 16th was our last day. Sob! Our flight wasn't until 7.30 p.m., so we had most of the day to do last-minute shopping. I had to have another anti-clotting injection before the flight, but I didn't actually feel that one go in, which was good. We flew business class again, and were served hot chocolate and cookies, then early breakfast, and landed at Heathrow airport at 7 a.m. on Thursday.

It was great to get home and see Molly and Daizy. I had over 600 emails to read through! Mum unfortunately had a migraine, so spent the next three days in bed, and it also took me a while to get over the jet lag! I had an absolutely brilliant time in New York, and would love to go back one day. Maybe next time I'll get to feel King Kong!

It was a fantastic treat to get away for a while and the atmosphere in America was lovely. It was relaxing and we got to enjoy some warm weather, although it was a little too hot sometimes – in the nineties! I'd definitely recommend going though.

Prince Charming

After New York, it was time to start ticking off the list of people I'd like to meet, and what a way to start!

On 14th October I went to Clarence House for a private audience with Prince Harry!

It was my second visit to Clarence House as I had been there a couple of months earlier to arrange an abseil with Prince Harry. Back in April when I won a Rotary young citizen award and was asked about my wish list, part of my answer was, 'I'd like to meet Prince Harry 'cause I like a rebel.' The BBC sent that to Prince Harry and told him about me and my upcoming abseil. He said he'd like to help me with it, but unfortunately he was too busy on the day that I did it. So I went to an office in Clarence House in August where his secretary, press officer and security tried to organise another one for us. We were struggling to find a place to do the abseil, and my suggestion of Big Ben was out of the question! It was then decided that the abseil would distract from my wish to meet Prince Harry, so the next day Clarence House phoned Mum and said that the prince had invited me to a private audience with him instead. I had to keep all of this a secret for months – you can imagine how difficult that was – but I was adamant it wasn't to get out in case it was cancelled.

I couldn't believe that 14th October finally arrived. It seemed like such a long way away back in the summer when it was being arranged. I was very excited and slightly nervous beforehand. We arrived early at Clarence House (better to be early than late!), so we were allowed to park our car in their car park next to the princes' cars, then we went for a walk around the park and Buckingham Palace. Mum, Nikki, my guide-communicator, and I then went to the private part of Clarence House where we met Prince Harry's private secretary. Then Prince Harry joined us. It was just the five of us and it was lovely. I got to spend over an hour and a half with him, which was an hour longer than planned, but we had a lot to talk about! I'm keeping private what was said though – sorry! All I will say is don't believe everything you read about Prince Harry (apart from this of course!). He's one of the nicest, funniest, most down-to-earth people I've ever met and gets way too much stick for no reason. It really cheered me up to meet him, and I have some lovely photos of us now.

Next to 'tick off' was my own documentary. This aired on Valentine's Day 2009, and was called *Our World: Nicole's Story*. I had filmed it with the BBC for ten months, and it covered my abseil, trip to New York, visiting a Teenage Cancer Trust unit, giving a speech at Arsenal football club and lots more. It was half an hour long and was shown six times over the weekend on the BBC News Channel. I had a great response, and received lots of donations for Nicole's Fund, which was brilliant. My main aim from the documentary was to raise awareness of Teenage Cancer Trust, and it certainly did that so I was pleased.

Wobbling on the cobbles

On 4th June 2009, I ticked off another thing – to 'wobble on the cobbles' at Coronation Street! We travelled to Manchester on the Wednesday, and we stayed in a lovely five star apartment – we even got chocolates and a red rose on our pillows! You don't even get that at the Hilton! On the Thursday we went to Granada studios where Coronation Street is filmed. My visit was organised by Teenage Cancer Trust as they knew this was one of my wishes, and we spent an hour and a half at the studios. I 'wobbled on the cobbles' first of all, which was actually more wobbly than I thought it would be. Then I felt different parts of the street including the paperboy sign outside Rita's cabin. When we got there Mum said, 'Do you want to feel the paperboy?' Luckily I knew what she meant! I also felt Maxine's bench outside Audrey's salon and the stone cladding on the Duckworths' house. It was really interesting finding out how it all works – I didn't realise how fake everything is! After wobbling, we then went to the part of the set where they film inside, which included the Rovers, where I sat in one of the booths, felt the pumps behind the bar and felt Betty's hotpot. I felt Vera's urn with her ashes and Jack's prize pigeon (stuffed) in the Duckworths' living room, the Battersbys' couch, the realistic but fake meat in Ashley's butcher's, and went inside Rita's shop. I also met some of the cast around the street that were filming that day including Jack (David Platt), Helen (Gail Platt), Sue (Eileen Grimshaw) and Michelle (Tina Mcintyre). They were all really nice and we had a great time there. After Corrie, we went to Christie's Hospital to visit their Teenage Cancer Trust unit. That night we went out for cocktails. The building where the bar was was twenty-three storeys high, and had glass walls so you could see across Manchester. We could even see Coronation Street in the distance!

So here's that list now:

I want to:

Have hair down to my bra strap ☑

Be in an advert ☐

Be in *OK!* magazine ☑

Be a millionaire ☐

Wobble on the cobbles at Coronation Street ☑

Go sky-diving ☐

Do an abseil ☑

Walk in heels ☐

Go to New York ☑

Have my own documentary ☑

Publish a book ☑

Meet Prince Harry ☑

Lists

As you've probably already noticed, I'm a big fan of writing lists. A bit geeky I know, but hey, I've already admitted my Tetley addiction, so I might as well admit the rest!

I make lists all the time. They help me keep things organised and under control. I write them for different reasons. I have 'The List', which is the main one you've just read about, which I created when I was sixteen so that I had goals to aim towards.

I also make little lists for things I want to do that day or even that month, which helps me keep things in order and under control (most of the time), but they're not as fun as 'The List'.

Because I was reaching the end of my original list, I decided to update it as there are lots of new things I want to do. Here are the latest additions:

Go skiing ☐

Drive a race car ☐

Ride an elephant ☐

Become a designer of something ☐

Go to Harley Street ☐

Climb a mountain ☐

Own a pink diamond ☐

S E V E N

Stone Me

Although 2008 was a great year for me achieving things, I still had my health problems. Towards the end of 2007, I started to feel unwell. I often have days where I'm run down and feel rubbish, but then I feel better again. This time, however, I didn't feel better, and for the following year I felt like absolute crap.

At first I thought I had a urinary tract infection, but after taking antibiotics for several weeks and still not feeling better, I started to worry. My back was more sore than usual, and was doing the weird throbbing achy feeling which is a sign that my cancer's back. I was also feeling really tired, weak, sometimes sick and just didn't feel right, so I asked to have an MRI scan to check the tumours on my spine. I was quite surprised when the results came back normal and that I was still in remission. That was in January 2008, but I continued to feel ill, and as time went on I began to feel worse.

Some days I felt a bit better, but still never 100 per cent. Most days I felt awful. My back was so painful that I had to start taking strong painkillers for it because paracetamol didn't help. Sometimes I'd double up with the pain and it was so bad it would bring tears to my eyes. But like with my hearing, no one really seemed to care and it was so frustrating. I kept telling my local nurses that I wasn't feeling right, but nothing got done. As I keep saying, I know my own body, and I know when something's not right.

After another three months of feeling awful, I went back to the Royal Marsden Hospital and asked for another scan, and again it came back clear. Then three months after that, when we were still no further with finding out what was wrong, I asked for another scan. I think deep down I knew I didn't need this one, but I was just desperate to find an answer so that I could start feeling better.

I was getting more and more anxious and upset that something was going wrong, and that we might not find out what was wrong until it was too late. It was also during this time that I had lost my hearing and became deafblind, so I was trying to cope with that as well. Yet again, the results of the MRI scan came back fine. I was still 100 per cent in remission. Obviously brilliant news and it was what I really wanted to hear, but we had made no progress in finding out what was wrong with me.

Then shortly after that I visited my GP – the one who listened to me about my needle phobia. I explained to her my symptoms and told her exactly what I'd been telling the community nurses for almost a year, and she referred me for an ultrasound of my stomach. I had my liver, kidneys etc. checked and all were fine, but it looked as if I had a bladder stone. It was quite big and they said it wouldn't just appear at that size, and that it had probably been growing for a long time. I then had an X-ray, and that confirmed that I did have a bladder stone. Yet another rare condition, and according to the medical book, it usually occurs in men! So just typical for me to develop one! It was a major relief to find the cause of why I had been feeling so bad, but also really frustrating that such a simple test had found it. The ultrasound that I had done just before my chemo started in 2006 detected a small stone, but we were never told this, so basically it had been growing ever since then, which had been two years.

I saw an urologist the following month who said he would remove the stone, and that should make me feel better. A few weeks later I had the operation to remove it. It was an hour-long, which was a bit longer than the surgeon thought it would take, probably because the stone was bigger than he was expecting. It turned out to be the size of an egg! He said it was the biggest one he'd ever seen. Now why doesn't that surprise me?

The good news is that within a couple of weeks of having the stone removed, I was feeling much better. My back wasn't as sore and I didn't feel as ill. So all that bother because of a stone!

E I G H T

Viva la Diva!

I've been lucky enough to win quite a few awards over the years now. I don't do the things I do to win awards or get praise, I do it because I love it and I want to make a difference, but it's always nice when I do receive an award. I really appreciate it and it spurs me on to keep doing what I'm doing. I have a nice collection of trophies and certificates now! And over the past couple of years I've added a few more . . .

I've already talked about winning 'Britain's most inspiring fundraiser', which was an absolutely brilliant, top award to win. Before that, in February

2008, I won a 'Spirit of the Try Angle' Award. The Try Angle Award is given in Kent, where I live, to 11–18-year-olds who achieve in different categories such as bravery, triumph over adversity, fund-raising and being a young carer. I've won three of these awards since 2005, and the 'Spirit of the Try Angle' Award is an extra one given to eighteen of the 150 young people who win each year. I went to an award ceremony and received a lovely glass trophy. I then became part of the committee to organise the Try Angle Awards, and pick the winners each year. For the Try Angle award ceremony in 2008 and 2009, I gave the opening and closing speeches on the night. I love being so involved with the award, and I hope to continue with it in the future. A few months later I received a Kent Deaf Children's Society Award, for the category of Deaf Young Adult, which recognises deaf or hearing-impaired young adults who have made a positive contribution to the community. This made me smile because I had only been deaf for six months, but had already won this award!

In April 2008, I was one of five young people from the UK to receive a Rotary Young Citizen Award. The award ceremony was in Blackpool, and we spent the weekend there, which I loved because I went there when I was about six, so I have good memories of it. I remember looking at the big rollercoaster and wanting to go on it, but being told no because I was too small! I was hoping to go on it while we were there for the award ceremony, but unfortunately I still wasn't allowed to due to health and safety reasons. I went on a couple of other rides, though, at the Pleasure Beach, including a rocket that just shot you up in the air – so I still had fun! The award ceremony was filmed live by the BBC, and in front of an audience of about 3,000 people. I received a glass trophy, a framed certificate and £500, which I donated to the Silver Lining Appeal to help me reach my £30,000 target. It was after the ceremony was shown on TV that someone set up the 'Nicole Dryburgh fan club' on Facebook! I love it!

I won my first book award in November 2008 for *The Way I See It*. My book made the longlist of the YoungMinds Book Award along with fourteen other books, which were all reviewed by children and young people to determine which books made the shortlist of six – and luckily mind did! YoungMinds is the UK's leading young person's mental health charity and each of the books chosen raised awareness of young people growing up in difficult circumstances. I attended the award ceremony in London, where the winning book was announced. Unfortunately it wasn't mine, but I was then surprised with a special award: the children's choice award that was voted for by the children who had been reviewing my book. It meant a lot as I wrote my book for young people, so the fact that they liked it was great! Then a few months later, I won another award for my book! It was called the 1066 Book Award, and was voted for by schools in Sussex. *The Way I See It* also made the shortlist for the Lancashire Book of the Year Award. Twelve schools across the area of Lancashire took part to read and review a hundred books, and then vote for their favourite. Mine made it to the top ten, so even though it didn't win the overall award, I was still really pleased with how far it got!

On 10th February 2009, I won a Diana Award, in memory of Princess Diana, for my charity work. I went to the award ceremony at Number 11 Downing Street where I received a Diana Award badge and framed certificate, plus a lovely glass trophy which was a special award because I was the 25,000th winner since the Diana Award was set up ten years earlier. After receiving my award, I gave a speech and was then surprised with a lovely letter from Prince Harry, which he wrote because he wanted to tell me personally how delighted he was that I was receiving a Diana Award. It made the night even more special.

Then a few months after that, I won an Anne Frank Award, and spent the day in London for the award ceremony. We arrived at Penguin books (who publish Anne Frank's diary) at 11.30 a.m., and there we heard some speeches about the awards and had some lunch. We walked to Westminster Pier afterwards and went on a ninety-minute river tour, and then we went to the House of Commons where the award ceremony was held. There were four other winners of various ages, and one of them had survived nine concentration camps. My award was presented by Bee Klug MBE, co-founder of the Anne Frank Trust UK and a friend of Miep Gies who risked her life to help the Frank family while they were in hiding. She was also the person who found Anne's diary. Miep phoned Bee and said she'd like to give an award to mark her 100th birthday this year and wanted it to go to someone with as much determination as Anne. As I had been nominated for an award this year, Bee read my story and decided I should get the special Miep

Award. Also at the award ceremony were Anne Frank's stepsister and the actress, Kate Ashfield, who played the part of Miep Gies in the mini-series on BBC1. If Anne had survived, she would have been eighty years old the day after the awards. I was presented with a lovely big glass trophy, and after the ceremony, we went to the House of Lords for a drinks reception.

And that's where the awards stop for now! I don't just grab the awards and run though, I try to stay involved with the people I've received them from and help if I can. I've already mentioned my involvement with the Try Angle Award, and I have a similar role with the Philip Lawrence Awards too. I won a Philip Lawrence Award in 2005, along with three other teenagers from Demelza House, for helping to design an adolescent room there. The following year I was involved in a sifting weekend to read through that year's entries for the award to wittle them down to a shortlist of twenty, all young people who had made an outstanding difference to their communities. At that weekend I was voted to be on the judging panel to pick the final winners, and I now take part in the judging process every year. Also on the panel is Frances Lawrence, the widow of Philip, Sir Trevor Macdonald, Kathryn, the Duchess of Kent and some other past winners like me. It can be very hard choosing the winners, and not everyone agrees on the same projects, but I enjoy it. I'm now quite experienced in giving speeches too. A few months after winning my Diana Award I gave a speech at another Diana Award ceremony where around eighty young people were presented with an award, and I've now been to several different Rotary clubs to talk about receiving my Rotary Young Citizen Award. It's nice to be so involved, and interesting to find out what goes on 'behind the scenes' with events like award ceremonies.

N   I   N   E

Dare 2 B Different?

When you consider the word 'different', what do you think? Is it a good word to you, or does it scare you? As ridiculous as it sounds, it used to kind of scare me, but now I love it, and I'm drawn to someone or something that's different, or to use another word, unique.

When I was younger and at school, I wanted to be like everyone else. I wanted to act the same, wear the same clothes, go to the same places etc. I didn't want to stand out or be different because I thought if I did everything the same as everyone else, it would mean I'd fit in and people would like me and not be bitchy towards me. It doesn't work like that, though, and whoever you are, and whatever you're like, there are always going to be people who don't like you, so you might as well be who you want to be, and not who you think you should be. It's only now that I'm older that I realise this and see how stupid it all is. But it's all part of growing up, I suppose, and learning from your experiences.

Therefore, I would urge everyone to be different, and proud of who you are. Be original and unique. Be who you want to be and don't care what other people think. I used to care too much about that, and it's really not worth it. I'm glad now that I'm different and I stand out. I wouldn't have won those awards I just wrote about if I wasn't who I am, so for that I'm grateful.

But if the word 'different' is still scaring you, think of it this way. Do celebrities all head down to New Look and buy the same dress in the same colour? No, they go for one-off vintage or designer collections that no one else has. That's so they stand out and aren't forgotten. Also so that they don't end up on the 'worst dressed' or 'what the hell was she thinking' list in a glossy magazine! I'd love to wear vintage dresses, only I can't afford them, and I don't like my legs! Hopefully you get what I'm trying to say from all this!

Of course, it's not all about fashion, as shocking as that might sound. It's the person underneath that counts. Your clothes are just a way of expressing who you are and showing your personality. It's about being true to yourself at the end of the day and being happy, so go on, dare 2 B different. You might enjoy it!

Be . . .

Be yourself – you are who you are. You can't change, so don't try to.

Be honest – always. By this I don't just mean handing a purse you've found into the police station or something like that (but obviously you should), I mean be honest with yourself. If you don't like something, or aren't happy, then say; it'll make your life a lot easier, and people will, or should, respect you for that.

Be original – it's the best way. People always remember 'the first', the rest after that just fade into the background.

Trust . . .

Trust the voice within – it talks a lot of sense. It knows you better than you might realise.

Trust your instincts – they're hardly ever wrong. There's times when I didn't trust mine and then regretted it, so I always go with my instincts now.

Trust me . . . I know what I'm talking about!

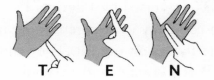

T E N

Dreams Can Come True

On 27th August 2008, my ultimate dream came true – I held a monkey! This has been my dream since I was eleven. I have been in love with monkeys ever since I picked up a leaflet for Monkey World while I was having eight weeks of daily radiotherapy at the Royal Marsden Hospital, to treat my cancer the first time round. There was a rack of leaflets advertising places to visit, and I would pick a load up to give me something to read on the four-hour car journey to and from the hospital. I was fascinated by the one about Monkey World, and it then became my dream to go there and hold a monkey.

I didn't think I'd ever be allowed to hold a monkey, so I was excited when I was told I could. The day was organised by Pilgrims Productions, a production company who were filming me tick off some of the things on my list. They contacted my local zoo, Port Lympne, and they said they had a baby monkey that they were hand rearing at the time, and that they were happy for me to go there and hold him. Woooooohooooo! He was a four-and-a-half-month-old Diana monkey called Keymon (an anagram of monkey), and was soooooooo cute! He looked like Marcel from *Friends*, black with white bits, really small with a long tail. I think his tail was actually longer than him!

The keeper carried him out cuddling a gorilla teddy, and he was quite shy at first, but within a minute, he was jumping all over me! His hands were just like babies' hands, and he kept grabbing *my* hands and shaking them. He would walk up and down my arms, and sit in both my hands if I held them out – I absolutely loved it! I think he liked me because I was kind of like a little platform for him to jump on to from the keeper's arms, then on to the ground, then back on me and to the keeper again!

I got to spend about twenty minutes with him, and it was brilliant. It really cheered me up, and it just shows, dreams really can come true.

In my last book, I mentioned that I wanted to have a zoo of adopted animals, and since 2008, there have been many animals strutting their stuff through the pink sparkly gates of my zoo! It's a unique zoo, which includes a tiger, panda, two elephants (got to love those big-nosed fellas), a monkey, two dogs and a swan. Most of these have been adopted for me as presents, as people know my passion for animals. I love having an adopted zoo. It's my way of having more animals which I love, without having them in the house and Mum moaning about them! I hope the zoo continues to grow and gets even more random!

Ambitions and goals

This is just a small section to encourage you to follow your dreams, because as I just proved, they really can come true.

Your dreams and goals should be personal to you whatever they are. Everybody has different things that they want to achieve. One person's dream could be another person's nightmare – not everyone would want to hold a monkey, but to me it meant the world and it was a personal ambition of mine.

If you really want to do something, then don't stop until you've done it. Anything is possible if you believe it enough – trust me on that one. The amount of times I could have given up on getting my first book published, but I didn't. I kept reminding myself that it was my dream, and to persevere. Whenever there was a setback, or I felt people didn't think it would ever be published, I let that drive me even more, and the feeling I got when it was finally published, and I held my book in my hands for the first time, was amazing, and worth all the hard work.

Five ways to reach your goals:

1. Set your goal firmly in your mind. Now that it's there, don't stop until you've achieved it.

2. Think about all the little steps you need to do to reach it. Why not write a list! Come on, it's fun – see, I'm doing it right now!

3. Start doing the steps towards reaching it. It may take you a while, even several years, but you'll get there in the end.

4. Never, ever give up on it. It'll happen if you believe it enough. The harder something

seems and the more you have to work makes the end achievement even better.

5. This is the most important one, have determination. That's what will get you to reach your goal.

Good luck!

You won't succeed

As I mentioned earlier, I love to write, and I write songs and poems. This is a poem I wrote when I was sixteen, and I originally wrote it about my cancer. I now read it as if it's aimed at anything that I'm struggling with, and it helps. It reminds me that I can get through anything, and to not let anyone, or anything, beat me, so here it is . . .

Standing strong
To prove you wrong
You won't succeed in breaking me.

I'll fight whatever you throw
So have a go

You won't succeed in breaking me.

I stand tall
Throughout it all
You won't succeed in breaking me.

Through thick and thin
I wear a grin
You won't succeed in breaking me.

You mean nothing to me
Just like it should be
You won't succeed in breaking me.

I thank you
For what you do
Coz you made me me.

E L E V E N

Author extraordinaire

I couldn't have asked for a better response to my first book *The Way I See It* (TWISI). Before it was published and 'on the shelves', I had no idea what to expect and was a bit worried that people wouldn't enjoy it, but I rarely have a day when I don't receive an email or comment from someone who has read it. Luckily, all have been very complimentary! The response from young girls has been amazing, and it means a lot to me that so many of them have called me their idol or role model. I wrote the book for young people, to give hope to others and also make people appreciate what they've got, and it's definitely done that from the reaction I've had. Some of the messages I've received have been very moving, and people have said my book has helped them understand things that they didn't before, or overcome something similar, so I'm really glad it's able to have that effect.

Doing book signings after TWISI was published was great fun. It made me feel like a proper author! I had my first one at my local Waterstone's store. I was really scared that no one would turn up, but luckily a good crowd did! I enjoyed meeting my 'fans' and signing my books for them. TWISI has also been a great success in schools, and I've been invited to several different schools now to meet the pupils. Often I give a talk in assembly in front of the school, so my public speaking is getting to be a full-time job now! It's great to meet the readers of my book, even if it does feel a bit strange to be back at school!

Writing *Talk to the Hand* has been quite different to writing *The Way I See It*. For a start, I'm several years older so my views and writing style have changed. I wrote most of TWISI when I was fifteen, when I first began to write, but I've gained a lot more experience in writing since then. In a

Nicole at a book event at Waterstone's

way this book has been easier because of that. I felt this book was needed to show that I'm still going strong, and I had so many people ask me to write another book that I didn't want to let them down!

Life as a working girl!

After fund-raising for Teenage Cancer Trust for a year – they offered me a job! Of course, I accepted straight away, and I love working for the charity. My official title is 'Regional fund-raiser – South East', and my job basically involves what I've been doing for years anyway – organising events to raise money, raising awareness of the charity, going to events to give speeches, supporting other people with fund-raising – only now I do a lot more of it. I love it! I even have my own little business cards! I mainly work from home, on my sexy pink laptop, but then I also go out to events too. I really enjoy working so closely with other people involved with TCT and I love being part of the team. I don't think I could have been offered a more perfect job. I can now help to make an even bigger difference to other young people fighting cancer.

Believe in miracles

This is one of my favourite sayings. I've loved it ever since Mum bought me a wooden angel holding a sign saying 'believe in miracles', when I came home from spending three months in hospital after my brain haemorrhage. I kept it at the end of my bed for years, and it's still in my room now with my other angels. I think it marked the start of my spiritual side. I always think of the saying, because for a miracle to happen, you have to believe in it, and as I found out in April 2009, they really can happen.

It had been two years since my chemo had finished, and I had an MRI scan to check I was still in remission. The results showed that I was, and I asked my oncologist what the chances were of me relapsing again. He said that he can't promise me, but he thinks that I might now be cured. Not words I ever expected to hear, but the best I ever will. It took a long time for the news to sink in, and it seemed like a miracle really had happened, but I just couldn't believe it!

My future is now very positive. I don't feel like I have a time limit any more, and I can plan things for the distant future because I now have one. It's such a great feeling, although I'll never lose the fear at the back of my mind that I'll relapse again. That's one of the effects of having cancer: once you've had it, you never lose the fear of it coming back. Mum came up with a saying after we heard the news, which I like: 'I live to live, not live to die.' Before, I lived my life to the full because I knew my life was going to be short. Now, I live my life to the full because I know how precious life is so I want to appreciate every minute of it. I've been given more than a second chance, I'm not going to waste it.

I have no idea what the future will hold for me now, but I look forward to it all: the good, the bad, the happy and the sad. I have lots of things I want to do, especially with my writing and charity work. I've been lucky enough to achieve a lot of the things I set out to, but personally, I think my biggest achievement is not letting my cancer succeed in breaking me. What a miracle!

Glossary

Bladder Stone

Stones can form in the bladder when waste products crystallise. Bladder stones can stop urine flowing freely from the bladder or can scratch away at the internal surface of the bladder, causing irritation and sometimes infection.

Cannula

A tube that is inserted into a blood vessel, organ or duct, to inject or remove fluid.

Chemotherapy (Chemo)

A method to treat cancer by using a chemical substance that destroys cancerous tissue.

Coma

A state of deep, often prolonged unconsciousness, usually as a result or an injury or disease, it is like a very long, deep sleep.

Engorged   When a blood vessel or tissue is
                        filled up or swollen with fluid.

Hickman line   A long hollow tube made from
                        silicone rubber that is inserted into
                        a major vein. It can be used for
                        taking blood tests and for giving
                        chemotherapy.

Intravenously   When a substance (e.g. a drug or
                        nutrient solution) is injected into
                        the body via a vein.

MRI scan   Stands for magnetic resonance
                        imaging. A type of scan that takes
                        detailed pictures by using magnets
                        and radio waves.

Neurofibromatosis   A hereditary condition that mainly
                        affects the nervous system and
                        causes tumours to grow on nerves
                        throughout the body. There are
                        two types of the disease. NF1 is
                        the most common type and NF2 is

generally the more serious.

Neuro-rehabilitation   A complex medical process which aims to aid recovery from a nervous system injury, such as a severe spinal injury or brain damage and to minimise and/or compensate for any functional problems resulting from it.

Occupational Therapy   Therapy using practical, purposeful activity to help individuals with physical and psychiatric conditions to cope independently in everyday life.

Oncologist   A doctor who specialises in the treatment of cancer.

Paediatrician   A doctor who specialises in treating children.

Peripheral Nerve   Made up of tumours that develop

Sheath Tumour	from the nerves outside the brain or spinal cord (the peripheral nerves). Those who have inherited neurofibromatosis are at greater risk of developing PNST.
Relapsed	The return of signs and symptoms of cancer after a period of remission.
Remission	A word that doctors often use in connection with cancer meaning that there is no sign of it. This does not mean to say that it is 'cured' as it can come back later.
Radiotherapy	A treatment of cancer by using X-rays.
Stroke	This happens when a blood clot forms that cuts off the blood supply to part of the brain or when a blood vessel bursts and bleeds into the brain.

Tinnitus	A symptom associated with many forms of hearing loss, usually distinguished by a ringing or roaring sound in the ears, occurring all the time or only occasionally. It can make it difficult to work, sleep and hear.
Ultrasound	A way of producing pictures of inside the body using sound waves.
Urologist	A doctor who specialises in bladder and urine problems.
Valium	Medication used to treat anxiety, seizures, insomnia and muscle spasms.
VQ Scan	VQ stands for Ventilation Quotient. It is a test that measures air and blood flow in your lungs.

Charities

I ended my last book with some of my favourite charities, and here are some more that I now support.

The Dogs Trust

If ever there was a charity that lived in my heart, this would be it. The Dogs Trust was set up in 1891, and was formerly known as the National Canine Defence League (NCDL). It is the UK's largest dog welfare charity, rescuing abandoned and neglected dogs. They never put a healthy dog down, and are dedicated to improving the lives of our four-legged friends.

In February 2008, Molly and Daizy made it on the shortlist for the Dogs Trust honours, in the hero dog category. It was a new award ceremony launched that year to recognise what dogs do for people, and is like the doggy Oscars. I nominated Molly and Daizy for the support they've given me over the years because I wouldn't have been able to get through it without them. So I was so pleased that they made it to the shortlist of five dogs. There were four other categories, and the hero dog category's winner was voted for by the readers of the *Sun* newspaper. We went to a posh award ceremony in London (Molly and Daizy included!), where we arrived along a yellow carpet with paw prints on! The winning dogs were announced on the night, but unfortunately Molly and Daizy didn't win. It didn't matter though because they're still my little hairy heroes! The really brilliant thing about the awards was that my editor came along with me to the ceremony. She hadn't heard of the charity before, but was inspired by the night and had the idea of publishing a book about the Dogs Trust. That book is now out to buy! It's called

Poppy the Dogs Trust Dog: A Dog is for Life. It's a great book and proceeds from it go to the Dogs Trust, so please buy a copy!
www.dogstrust.org.uk

Teenage Cancer Trust

Teenage Cancer Trust (TCT) is a charity devoted to improving the lives of teenagers and young adults with cancer. Their main aim is to build special state-of-the-art units in NHS hospitals for 13–24-year-olds going through treatment for cancer. The units are designed to have a homely atmosphere, and are full of things that teenagers like, such as games consoles, internet access, pool tables, satellite TV, plus a music room, chill-out room, games room, kitchen to avoid hospital food and lots more. So far, TCT have nine units across the UK, and their aim is to build another fourteen by 2012, so that every young person going through treatment for cancer has access to one of these units.

As I mentioned earlier, every day in the UK, six teenagers and young adults are diagnosed with cancer. One in every 312 boys and one in every 361 girls gets cancer before they're twenty. Teenagers contract some of the rarest and most aggressive types of cancer, and the survival rate falls well below that of other age groups. There are now more teenagers living with cancer than there are children with cancer. These are the facts that make me so passionate about helping Teenage Cancer Trust. **www.teenagecancertrust.org**

Nicole's Fund

Nicole's Fund is something I've set up with Teenage Cancer Trust. It is an honour to have a fund set up with such a great charity, and it's something very close to my heart. I set up Nicole's Fund so that the money I raise for Teenage Cancer Trust goes specifically towards building the TCT unit at the Royal Marsden Hospital in Sutton, Surrey. This hospital treats people of all ages from across Kent, Surrey and Sussex. It's a very special hospital to me and that's why I set the fund up to help build the much needed teenage unit there. **www.justgiving.com/nicolesfund**

Sense

Sense is the leading national charity that supports and campaigns for deafblind children and adults. It was founded in 1955 as 'the rubella group', but changed its name to Sense in 1983. It was set up as a self-help and support group for the parents of children whose disabilities were neither recognised nor provided for. The children were born deafblind as a result of their mothers catching rubella during pregnancy. When Sense was first established, their main priority was to set up a newsletter, which is still going strong today as a magazine called *Talking Sense*. Since the summer of 2008, I have written a column for *Talking Sense*, sharing my life as a young deafblind person.

Today, Sense is the UK's largest voluntary-sector provider of services to people with sight and hearing difficulties. They employ over 1,500 staff, meeting the needs of thousands of deafblind people from babyhood to old age.

www.sense.org.uk

Deafblind Manual Alphabet

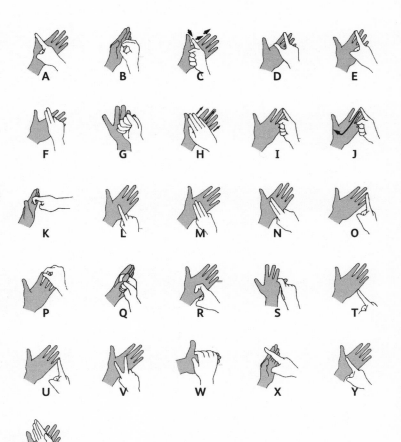

Acknowledgements

This is my chance to say some special *thank you*s to the people who continue to stand by me and support me:

Firstly, Mum, Lee, Molly and Daizy – love you! xxx

My friends – you know who you are! x

My TCT family – Helen and the rest of the South East team, plus everyone else who does such a brill job. Thank you for this amazing opportunity! xx

Nikki – oh the fun we've had and the places we've parked the Noo mobile! 'Love it!' Thank you for being such a great support. xx

Jules – thanks for all the fab pics!

My loyal fundraising supporters – without your kind and generous donations over the years, I wouldn't have been able to reach my fundraising targets. I'm very grateful for that, so thank you.

Everyone who helped me 'tick' something off of my wish list. You helped make some of my biggest dreams come true – thank you!

TEENAGE CANCER TRUST

HELPING YOUNG PEOPLE
FIGHT CANCER

Registered Charity Number: 1062559

Please help make a difference to young people fighting cancer by donating to Nicole's Fund in aid of Teenage Cancer Trust at:

www.justgiving.com/nicolesfund

Or send a cheque made payable to Teenage Cancer Trust to:

Teenage Cancer Trust
Nicole's Fund
93 Newman Street
London
W1T 3EZ

If you would like any more information, or are interested in organising an event to raise money for Nicole's Fund, then please contact me on:

nicole.dryburgh@teenagecancertrust.org

I will be adding different fundraising events regularly to the fundraising page on my website, so please keep checking www.c-h-o-c.org.uk to see how you can get involved. Thank you!

Read Nicole's inspiring story of her fight to rebuild her life after cancer - a moving, funny and unforgettable story of a refusal to give up hope.

'This story is truly inspirational but also accessible and deals with the harsh reality of life with cancer in straight forward way.' Write Away

'Nicole's inspirational story will leave anyone who reads it in utter awe of her selflessness, sense of humour and incredibly positive outlook in the face of such immense and extreme obstacles.' Waterstone's Books Quarterly

'An amazing story of courage and triumph over adversity.' Chicklish

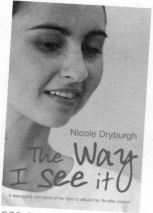

Nicole Dryburgh

The Way
I see it

978 0 340 95692 2

'I felt like I was in the room with Nicole and she was telling me her story. She is an excellent example of not giving up.' Olivia, Year 9

'After reading it she is now my hero.'
Charlotte, Year 9

'This is an incredible story told in a refreshingly honest way ... It is truly an engrossing read; you engage with Nicole from the first page and don't want to put her story down.' Hackwriters

Another *Hodder Children's Book*

POPPY THE DOG'S TRUST DOG
A dog is for life . . .

By Sophia Fergus

Poppy was born in the Dogs Trust rehoming centre on Merseyside. The shoe-sized puppy was happily rehomed, but just two weeks later, Poppy became seriously ill and was rushed straight to the vet's. She was still so tiny that she might not survive . . .

Here are the heartwarming and unforgettable stories of Poppy the Dogs Trust office dog and some of the thousands of other dogs rescued by the Trust.

A dog is for life, not just for Christmas.

h HODDER

Another *Hodder Children's Book*

WEIGHING IT UP
A teenager's frank account of her struggle with anorexia

By Ali Valenzuela

Currently 1.15 million people in the UK have an eating disorder.

'I want people to understand that there is more to anorexia than looking thin; the thin appearance is only a physical outcome of the pain and torment that goes on inside.

'I feel open to talking about my experience, as it may help other people. Just because I went through a difficult struggle doesn't mean that something positive annot come of it.'

Ali Valenzuela's frank account of being anorexic includes diary extracts from the point when, at age 14, the illness started to control her life, to the present-day when she is controlling the illness.